CW01149914

Jonah and Nahum Prophetic Messengers to the Assyrian City of Nineveh

An Expositional Commentary

ANDRE T. HIBLER

Order this book online at www.trafford.com
or email orders@trafford.com

Most Trafford titles are also available at major online book retailers.

© Copyright 2024 Andre T. Hibler.

All rights reserved. No part of this publication may be reproduced, stored in a retrieval system, or transmitted, in any form or by any means, electronic, mechanical, photocopying, recording, or otherwise, without the written prior permission of the author.

Print information available on the last page.

ISBN: 978-1-6987-1828-6 (sc)
ISBN: 978-1-6987-1829-3 (hc)
ISBN: 978-1-6987-1830-9 (e)

Library of Congress Control Number: 2024923882

Because of the dynamic nature of the Internet, any web addresses or links contained in this book may have changed since publication and may no longer be valid. The views expressed in this work are solely those of the author and do not necessarily reflect the views of the publisher, and the publisher hereby disclaims any responsibility for them.

Scripture quotations taken from the (NASB®) New American Standard Bible®, Copyright © 1960, 1971, 1977, 1995 by The Lockman Foundation.
Used by permission. All rights reserved. www.lockman.org

Any people depicted in stock imagery provided by Getty Images are models, and such images are being used for illustrative purposes only.
Certain stock imagery © Getty Images.

Trafford rev. 11/18/2024

Trafford www.trafford.com
North America & international
toll-free: 844-688-6899 (USA & Canada)
fax: 812 355 4082

To **Jesus Christ**
who is the Resurrection and the Life
our complete justification
the Ultimate Superlative One who surpasses all others

Preface

Four common features of God consistent throughout the Bible are underscored in Jonah and Nahum: love, compassion, mercy, and judgment. These four characteristics are the direct aim of one gentile city—Nineveh, the capital of Assyria. Love, compassion, and mercy relate to Jonah, whereas judgment pertains to Nahum. Jonah and Nahum were never written as one prophetic book and later separated into two independent historical records, such as 1 and 2 Samuel, 1 and 2 Chronicles, 1 and 2 Kings, and Ezra and Nehemiah. However, Nahum's prophecy—the later book—corresponds and correlates to Jonah. In approximately 780 BC, Jonah proclaimed to Nineveh a message of impending calamity contingent on its repentance (Jon. 3:4-10). Just more than a century later (663-612 BC), Nahum declared an exterminatory judgment on the great city to include the entire nation of Assyria (Nah. 2:13; 3:5-7).

The book of Jonah regards the Lord's revelatory sovereign power and loving compassion for people and animals (Jon. 4:11). This disclosure was not solely for the Ninevites, but for Jonah and the Israelites. The Assyrians were responsible for repentance and humility. The nation obeyed Jonah's message (Jon. 3:6-10). Israel—when faced with threats from Assyria and Babylon and that was guilty before the Lord of idolatry, violence, hypocritical ritualism, social injustice, and spiritual apathy—should have shared the same penitence and modesty that the Assyrians did. Yet, despite its sins, Israel was not moved toward repentance. Jonah's repudiation and lack of concern for the Ninevites contrast with the Lord's affection for them. Jonah's purpose was to instruct the Israelites that the Lord loves and cares for nations other than their own. Israel should have modeled its sovereign Lord by expressing the same sentimentality for other nations that He does.

Nineveh repented at Jonah's proclamation, and the Lord exercised mercy, to renounce the calamity He initially declared on the foreign nation. It is presumed that the Assyrians treasured the Lord's grace. If so, their appreciation for the Lord's forgiveness faded within a century. In 722 BC, the Assyrians decimated the ten tribes of the Northern Kingdom of Israel and had the Southern Kingdom of Judah in view. The Assyrians destroyed many Judean cities and even unsuccessfully besieged Jerusalem in 701 BC. The tribe of Judah, though, remained until 586 BC, when exiled to Babylon in the third and final deportation. In effecting control of the former Northern Kingdom, the Assyrians exiled many Israelites, and either Shalmaneser V or Sargon II transported in Assyrian people and repatriated them to inhabit the Samarian region. While numerous Israelites were exiled, others remained in the area and intermarried with the Assyrians. The progeny of these biracial marriages became known as the Samaritans. Because of their mixed-raced ethnicity, the Jews of the intertestamental and the young New Testament era did not recognize the Samaritans as authentic Israelites, nor did they hold them in high regard. In fact, the Jews despised them.

The Assyrians were known for exerting domineering power and excessive savagery to subjugate other nations. These elements are not commensurate with the graciousness of the Lord that He exhibited to them through Jonah. The Lord initially forgave the Ninevites and, inside a hundred years, the nation of Assyria devastated Israel. Aside from its malicious and oppressive appetite, three theoretical reasons may have stimulated Assyria to destroy Israel. First of all, the initial generation did not communicate its repentance to the subsequent generation and so on. Second, if the initial generation disseminated the Lord's grace to the succeeding generations, it may have been ignored or spurned. Third, the Assyrians simply rescinded their repentance. Regardless of the motive, the Assyrians' actions infuriated the Lord. Thus, the Lord, through Nahum's prophecy, declared an oracle judgment on Nineveh and the entire Assyrian nation.

The Lord's anger grew out of the love for His people. His love is the surety of His wrath. Although Israel was guilty before the Lord, and Assyria was an agent of chastisement against the Lord's mutinous and wayward people, Yahweh holds the gentile nation corporately responsible for the immoderations and carnages committed in fulfilling this role of destruction (Isa. 10:7-19; Zep. 2:13-15). Nahum's announcement of judgment (Nah. 2:13; 3:5-7) and woe oracle (Nah. 3:1-4) enable or urge Judah to rejoice (Nah. 1:15; 3:19). In 612 BC, Nahum's prophecy came to realization when the Medo, Babylonian, and Scythian alliance obliterated the city of Nineveh, which signified the end of the Assyrian Empire.

The Lord had sympathy for Assyria just as He does for other gentile nations. But His anger toward Assyria emanated from the love He held for His elect: namely, Israel. The barbaric Ninevites, on whom the Lord showed compassion, destroyed the ten northern tribes of Israel, whom He called His own and redeemed from Egyptian bondage (Exod. 6:7). In keeping the Abrahamic covenant, the Lord will not tolerate mistreatment of His people (Gen. 12:3). Love and wrath were designated for one gentile nation, yet the Lord is proper in His actions.

Contents

Preface vii

JONAH

Author and Background 1
Chapter 1 9
Chapter 2 27
Chapter 3 38
Chapter 4 47

NAHUM

Author and Background 61
Chapter 1 69
Chapter 2 79
Chapter 3 86

Bibliography 97

JONAH

Author and Background

The name Jonah *(Yonoh)* means *dove*. Although the writer does not speak in the first person, Jonah, the son of Amittai from the tribe of Zebulun, is identified as the author (1:1). He was a native of Gath-hepher (near Nazareth); his ministry occurred during the long reign of Jeroboam II (ca. 793-753 BC [2 Kings 14:25]). During the time of the divided kingdom, Gath-hepher was a town in Zebulun in Northern Israel. In the New Testament era, Zebulun, which was a part of Palestine, was the region of Galilee. Hence, the Pharisees were in error when they mentioned "that no prophet arises out of Galilee" (John 7:52).

Regarding the Bible's table of contents, Jonah is the fifth of the Minor Prophets. Those prophets not credited for writing a book—Elijah (1 Kings 17-19) and Elisha (2 Kings 2:1-13:21)—and Scripture-ascribed prophets—Obadiah (ca. 848 BC) and Joel (ca. 835 BC)—precede Jonah. He is the only prophet who was sent to a cruel gentile nation to preach a message of repentance. Jonah was Israel's alien missionary; Hosea was Israel's household missionary. Hosea revealed that the Lord still has a vibrant loyal love for Israel despite its infidelities. The book of Jonah disclosed that the Lord has compassion for all gentile nations, including the fierce Ninevites of Assyria.

Following the death of King Adad-nirari III in 783 BC, it is quite plausible that the Assyrian Empire, during this era, was debilitated. The nation did not become formidable again until Tiglath-pileser III seized the throne in 745 BC. Within this thirty-eight-year period, Assyria struggled against neighboring forces—Mannai, Madai, and the Urartu tribe—to the north. These allied invaders pushed the northern border of Assyria to the south within a hundred miles of Nineveh. Because its army had lost ground, Assyria was heavily challenged, weakened, and seemingly vulnerable. This factor may have served as a presage of God's divine wrath. Because of this condition, the king and the residents may have deemed it practical to receive and adhere to Jonah's message—which may have been substantiated by his profitless gain concerning his mission and his foreign ethnicity. With Nineveh's perceivable demise in view, the people repented following Jonah's proclamation via the Lord.

DATE

Jonah commenced his ministry in approximately 780 BC.

PURPOSE

The book of Jonah exhibits the Lord's loving compassion for other nations, including animals (4:11). The Ninevites were not the sole recipients of the Lord's revelatory Word. This revelation was designated to Jonah personally and, through him, to the Jews. The city of Nineveh repented in obedience to the Lord's proclamation. This disclosure was an example for Israel to imitate the foreign nation's contrition and meekness. The Israelites encountered threats from the Assyrians and the Babylonians. Jonah's lack of regard for the Ninevites differs from the Lord's concern for them that was to be the paradigm for His people. The chief purpose of the book was to teach Israelites that the Lord loves other foreign nations just as His own; and the Israelites, with emulation of the Lord, should impart His sympathy to other nations, as well.

CHARACTERISTICS

Unlike most of the Old Testament prophetic books, Jonah is practically all narrative. There are no continuous oracle of judgments or repeated declarations. There is no esoteric language or any passages that are notably difficult to translate (e.g., Isa. 7:10-25; Eph. 2:11-22; Heb. 6:1-8; 10:26-39; James 2:14-26; Rev. 20:1-6). This is a book in which an elephant can swim, and a small child can splash. It is a story about the Lord sending His prophetic servant to a barbaric, gentile nation—on which He has compassion—in which He attempts to shape the heart of a prophet with enormous contempt for this nation and to give an example for the people of Israel. Ironically, the people of Nineveh repent at the hearing of Jonah's message. Yet, the Israelites lost their kingdom and eventually went into exile after being told to repeatedly repent—for more than three hundred years after the kingdom was divided—of their disobedience to God and the Mosaic covenant.

THEOLOGICAL THEME

Although an Israelite prophet, Jonah is not remembered for his ministry. Rather, the book communicates the narrative of his call to preach repentance to Nineveh and his rejection of God's mandate. It contains more of a record of Jonah's experience than his actual message. God dealt with Jonah more so than with Nineveh.

Nineveh, which was notorious for its barbarity, was a historical adversary of Israel and Judah. The emphasis of the book of Jonah pertains to that pagan city, founded by Nimrod, Noah's great-grandson (Gen. 10:6–12). Possibly the largest city in the archaic world (1:2;

3:2-3; 4:11), Nineveh was nonetheless demolished in 612 BC, or roughly 170 years after the repentance of the generation of Jonah's stay. Israel's abhorrence for Assyria, linked with a perception of spiritual preeminence as the recipient of God's covenant blessing, produced an obstinate defiance in Jonah toward God's charge for missionary service. Comparatively, God directed Jonah to Nineveh to dishonor Israel by the fact that a pagan city repented at the preaching of a foreigner, whereas Israel repudiated the preaching of repentance by many of their own prophets. God would show Jonah that His love, mercy, and graciousness encompass all His creatures (4:2, 11), not just His sovereign elect (Gen. 12:1-3).

As the sovereign choice of God, the Israelites sensed a characteristic of exclusivity. During the reign of Jeroboam II, Israel expanded geographically. The nation formed affiliations with neighboring nations, yet simultaneously maintained exclusive religiosity. The Israelites perceived that their privileged relationship with God needed protection from the gentiles, so that they would not take it from them as they had previously taken so many other things. The Israelites propelled this hostile attitude—an attitude that Jonah embodied—onto Yahweh; however, this was not so with God. In fact, God demonstrated compassion toward the Ninevites.

The book of Jonah discloses God's sovereignty over man and all creation and, more specifically, His compassion for Nineveh. "For from Him and through Him and to Him are all things. To Him be the glory forever. Amen" (Rom. 11:36). The Lord is the *source* from which "all things" originate ("from Him"); the *way* by which "all things" occur ("through Him"); and the *aim* toward which "all things" progress ("to Him"). He is similarly the Creator, sustainer, and finisher of everything conclusively.

In view of all these attributes, roles, and redemptive works, He deserves all "glory forever." Jonah knew the majesty and the awesomeness of God all too well but, because he hated Nineveh (4:1-3), God's empathy for Nineveh angered him.

To exemplify the hard hearts of the Pharisees and their lack of desire to repent, Jesus, interestingly enough, applied the repentance of the Ninevites to rebuke the Pharisees (Matt. 12:38–41; Luke 11:29–32). The infidel city of Nineveh repented at the preaching of a refractory prophet, but the Pharisees refused to repent at the preaching of the greatest of all prophets—Jesus Christ—in spite of the mounting evidence that He was their Lord. God designated and appointed Jonah, as a depiction of Israel, to be His witness (Isa. 43:10–12; 44:8).

NOTABLE THEME

Blessings to believers, and to others through believers, stem from obedience to the Lord. Discipline from the Lord is a result of disobedience.

KEY VERSE

"But I will sacrifice to You with the voice of thanksgiving. That which I have vowed I will pay. Salvation is from the Lord" (2:9).

ASSYRIAN CRUELTY

Nineveh was located on the eastern embankment of the Tigris River. The city walls were a hundred feet high and fifty feet wide, and the principal wall, interspersed by fifteen gates, was more than 7½ miles long. The total population was roughly six hundred thousand—including the people who lived on the outskirts, beyond the city walls (4:11). The idolatrous residents adored Asur and Ishtar, the primary male and female deities, as did most of the Assyrians. Assyria was a threat to Israel's security (Isa. 7:17; Hos. 9:3; 10:6-7; 11:5; Amos 5:27). This is one reason Jonah refused to go to Nineveh. He feared the people might repent, and the Lord would refrain from punishing Israel's enemy (4:2).

Jonah maintained full knowledge of Assyrian treachery. Although affiliated forces to the north ostensibly threatened Assyria's kingdom, Nineveh was still a strong host with which to be reckoned. Years prior to Jonah's ministry, Assyria was a rising, dominant world power destined to decimate Israel. Therefore, Jonah did not want the Lord to save, but destroy Nineveh.

Not only was Assyria a peril to the well-being of Israel, but the nation imposed extreme cruelty on those whom they conquered. History indicates that King Sennacherib's (704-681 BC) executioners tortured victims by holding them down and ripping their tongues out of their mouths. Men were pegged to the ground and flayed alive with a sharp knife. Their layers of skin would be displayed on the city walls to terrify people. Other sufferers would be impaled on poles and left to die. Men were blinded, had their eyes gouged out, and were deprived of their hands and feet. Ears and noses were cut off. Children were burned alive. Decapitated human heads were exhibited in a pyramid to indicate a conquest and to mark the path of a vanquisher. The men of Israel, especially Jonah, knew these things. In refusing to proclaim repentance to Nineveh, Jonah attempted to flee from the Lord (1:3).

Outline

I. **The Disobedient Prophet (1)**
   A. Jonah and the storm (1:1-17)
      1. The Lord commissions Jonah to go to Nineveh (1-2)
      2. Jonah attempts to flee from the Lord (3)
      3. Jonah lacks sympathy (4-6)
      4. Jonah acknowledges but does not fear the Lord's sovereignty (7-10)

5. The gentile sailors show compassion and fear the Lord (11-16)
6. The Lord appoints a great fish to swallow Jonah (17)

II. The Disciplined Prophet (2)
  A. Jonah and the fish (2:1-10)
  1. Jonah prays to the Lord from the belly of the fish (1)
  2. Jonah's psalm of thanksgiving, contrition, and rededication (2-9)
  3. The Lord delivers Jonah from the fish (10)

III. The Dynamic Prophet (3)
  A. Jonah and Nineveh (3:1-10)
  1. The Lord recommissions Jonah to go to Nineveh (1-2)
  2. Jonah proclaims repentance to the Ninevites (3-4)
  3. The Ninevites repent (5-10)

IV. The Displeased Prophet (4)
  A. Jonah and the Lord (4:1-11)
  1. Jonah is disappointed and frustrated with the Lord's mercy (1-4)
  2. The Lord rebukes Jonah for his attitudinal sin (5-9)
  3. The Lord has sympathy for those subject to His judgment (10-11)

SUMMARY

The Lord commissioned Jonah to go to Nineveh to present a sermonic discourse of repentance and forgiveness to the wicked Ninevites (1:1-2). Much to his dismay, Jonah rebelled against the Lord and set sail for Tarshish (1:3), in the opposite direction from Nineveh, because he did not want the Lord to have mercy on a vile and ruthless people. Jonah's flight from the Lord resulted in a massive storm, which almost destroyed the ship and distressed the sailors. Jonah slept peacefully at the bottom of the ship. Its distraught captain awakened him to demand that he call on his God in an attempt to prevent them from dying. Jonah revealed to the men of the ship his ethnic identity and advised them that he was the root cause of this disastrous hurricane. At Jonah's suggestion, they reluctantly threw him into the sea to calm the storm but only after they hopelessly tried to return to land (1:4-16). The Lord assigned a fish to swallow Jonah (1:17).

While in the belly of the "great fish," Jonah prayed for deliverance, and the aquatic animal expelled him onto the dry land (2). The Lord recommissioned Jonah to deliver His message of repentance to the city of Nineveh (3:1-4). When the people repented, the Lord relented His judgment (3:5-10). Angered and disappointed by the Lord's mercy, Jonah sulked and was rebuked (4).

With extreme discontentment for the Ninevites, Jonah wanted the Lord to judge them, but His withdrawal from tragedy was for His own glory and not for Jonah's benefit. It was the Lord's prerogative to have mercy and compassion on Nineveh (Exod. 33:19; Rom. 9:18). Jonah's sole obligation was to answer the Lord's call and, without reservation, conduct himself in complete obedience.

EXPOSITION

CHAPTER 1

The word of the LORD came to Jonah the son of Amittai saying, (v. 1)

The phrase, "The word of the Lord came to," occurs more than one hundred times in the Old Testament. Jonah did not detail *how* he received the revelatory message from the Lord; instead, he stated it plainly. Albeit the method of revelation in other prophetic books is apparent, the *how* in Jonah is extraneous. The perplexing time of this revelation is dispensable to the interpretation and application of this book. The Lord's actions are the pertinent highlight in the prophetic message.

Amittai, the father of Jonah, means *loyal* and *true*. He lived in Gath-hepher (2 Kings 14:25). Other than the fact that Amittai was Jonah's father, there is no knowledge of him. Documenting the name of a significant person's father was a commonality in Jewish writings, and the mention of Amittai's name in the first verse of the text contends for the historical validity of Jonah.

Jonah means 'dove.' In a biblical context, dove can symbolize purity or absurdity:

We associate the dove with peace and purity; however, this positive meaning is not the only possible association. A 'dove' could also be a symbol of silliness (see Hos. 7:11), a description that sadly applies to this tragicomical prophet.[1]

Gath-hepher is a town in Zebulun (named after and allocated to Jacob's sixth son by his wife Leah but tenth son overall) located in Northern Israel. The region overlooks the Jezreel Valley to the south. Although the text is syntactically addressed in the third person ("came to Jonah"), Jonah is identified as the author. In the Palestinian New Testament era at the time of Jesus, Zebulun is the region of Galilee. Galilee is slightly north of Cana and Nazareth, formally the area of Issachar—named after and allotted to Jacob's fifth son by his wife Leah but ninth in total.

"Arise, go to Nineveh the great city and cry against it, for their wickedness has come up before Me" (v. 2).

The Lord commissioned Jonah to go to the great city of Nineveh to preach a message of repentance. Founded by Nimrod (Gen. 10:8-11), Nineveh, the "great city," was the capital city of the Assyrian Empire for many years. Surrounded by a circuit wall that stretched nearly eight miles, Nineveh stood on the east bank of the Tigris River across from the present-day Iraq, located in the city of Mosul. With its size, a population of more than a hundred thousand people could inhabit this "great city."

Jonah was to "cry against" Nineveh so much that the Lord was well-aware of its iniquities. He was not to identify the sins of the city but to announce repentance to the people, thereby eliminating their conditional judgment provided the Ninevites repent. As indicated

---

[1] *The Nelson Study Bible*, ed. Earl Radmacher (Nashville: Thomas Nelson Publishers, 1997), 1493.

in **Assyrian Cruelty**, the Ninevites (or Assyrians) were known for their unspeakable cruelness and brutality to others. They constituted a murderous, egregious regime, which was fortified with iron weaponry that enabled them to establish mass armies with war-fighting superiority. Their atrocities came before the Lord; consequently, He sanctioned Jonah to go to Nineveh to proclaim a message of repentance.

While other prophetic messengers prophesied to gentile nations—Obadiah to Edom and Nahum to Assyria (as well)—Jonah, in the Old Testament, is the only case in which the Lord actually sent one of His servants to a foreign nation as a missionary. The Ninevites might have regarded the outsider Jonah as a divine messenger and not some foreign detractor of their communitarian ethos. Because of Israel's contempt and envy—along with rebuke for its refusal to bring the gentiles to the Lord—provisional deliverance for Nineveh was in view.

But Jonah rose up to flee to Tarshish from the presence of the LORD. So he went down to Joppa, found a ship which was going to Tarshish, paid the fare and went down into it to go with them to Tarshish from the presence of the LORD (v. 3).

The second verse indicates a clear command from the Lord. The conjunctive word "but," the first word in this verse, denotes a contrariwise action of Jonah. With inductive insight and before one reads the rest of the passage, a reasonable act of disobedience can be inferred. However, before an implication can be fully speculated, "Jonah rose up to flee to Tarshish from the presence of the Lord." If disobedience was insinuated after observing the conjunction "but," yet prior to reading the entire verse, it was now a reality. Jonah in fact disobeyed the Lord.

Before I examine *why* Jonah disobeyed a direct command from the Lord, I want to highlight the rewards for Christians being in complete obedience to God. First of all, Jonah's attitude was incorrect and sinful. Obeying the Lord will be as pertinent to the Lord's servant as it is to the people to whom His servants minister. In obeying the Lord, we find sustenance (John 4:34), illumination (John 7:17), and empowerment (Heb. 13:21). These are fundamental elements that will grow God's people. To Jesus, obeying the will of God was satisfactory nourishment; to Jonah, obeying the will of God—as this instance is conveyed—was distasteful food. Nothing pleasurable comes from forsaking the Lord's will.

In refusing the Lord's will, Jonah decided to flee to Tarshish, a city or territory in southern Spain, approximately fifteen hundred to two thousand miles west of Joppa—which is modern-day Jaffa and a seaport on the Mediterranean Sea about thirty-five miles west of Jerusalem. Tarshish is the name of Noah's great-grandson via his son Japheth, through his son Javan (Gen. 10:1-4). The text describes the descendants of this individual and the area where they settled (1 Kings 10:22; 22:48; 1 Chron. 7:10). The tribe of Dan inherited the territory of Joppa (Josh. 19:46). Jonah attempted to travel as far as possible from the Lord, in the opposite direction from his designated destination in sheer reluctance to bring a proclamation of repentance to the Ninevites of Assyria.

Jonah knew about Assyria's brutality and that the nation was a huge threat to Israel's well-being (see **Assyrian Cruelty**). Assyria was Israel's enemy. In a patriarchal sense, Jonah may have fled to spare Israel from Assyrian devastation. Maybe he assumed that the Ninevites would incur the Lord's wrath if no saving message was delivered to them. From Jonah's perspective, delivering a salvific message to a menacing foe seemed to be an undesirable and objectionable task. Instead of Assyria and the city of Nineveh receiving the opportunity to repent, "Jonah would much rather see the city destroyed."[2] This one is another likely reason that he ran away from the Lord. But no one can escape the ubiquitousness and omnipresence of the Lord. "Jonah was obedient to deliver the message of blessing to Israel of expanding its borders (2 Kings 14:25), but not a message that could bless his enemies."[3] His patriotism superseded his theology. Peril exists in loving your own people more than the Lord. To love the Lord's people entirely is to trust and obey the Lord completely (1 John 5:1); and His counsel stands forever throughout generations (Ps. 33:11). Jonah's voluntary attempt to forfeit his prophetic office proved futile. Instead of finding the perfect ship waiting for him and paying the fare for his long journey, Jonah should have realized that the Lord loved both him and the Ninevites. Unlike a secular position, which one can vacate or terminate, Jonah's service unto the Lord is for a lifetime.

> An officer in an army may resign the commission of his president or king, but an ambassador of the Lord is on a different basis. His service is for life, and he may not repudiate it without the danger of incurring God's discipline.[4]

The LORD hurled a great wind on the sea and there was a great storm on the sea so that the ship was about to break up (v. 4).

The Lord divinely orchestrated the "great wind…and…great storm on the sea." He was at work amid the prodigal prophet. The "wind" and "sea" were purposely obedient. The Lord's goal was to bless the city

---

[2] Warren Wiersbe, *The Bible Exposition Commentary: Isaiah-Malachi* (Colorado Springs: David C. Cook, 2002), 378.

[3] Bill Thrasher, "Jonah," in *The Moody Bible Commentary*, ed. Michael Rydelnik and Michael Vanlaningham (Chicago: Moody Publishers, 2014), 1363.

[4] Frank E. Gaebelein, *Four Minor Prophets: Obadiah, Jonah, Habakkuk, and Haggai* (Chicago: Moody Press, 1970), 74.

of Nineveh. Yet Jonah's departure from the Lord brought about a curse and not a blessing. The Lord called the Jews to be a blessing to all the nations (Gen. 12:1-3) but, whenever the Jews were outside the Lord's will, trouble and calamity occurred. Twice Abraham invited distress to people because of his deception (Gen. 12:10-20; 20:1-18); Achan brought uneasiness to Israel's army because he robbed the Lord (Josh. 7); and Jonah caused great anxiety to pagan mariners because he fled from the Lord.

Although Jonah supposedly resigned from his prophetic duty, the Lord—for at least this particular point in time—spoke to Jonah in His works and not His words. The Lord produced a mighty wind with torrential rain, with the potential to eradicate a ship that transported the lives of innocent, gentile sailors and an insubordinate Hebrew prophet. The Lord's action indicated that Jonah's rebellious journey would soon end. Contemplate all that Jonah lost because of his refusal to bless others. "It was gracious of God to seek out His disobedient servant and not to allow him to remain long in his sin."[5]

Then the sailors became afraid and every man cried to his god, and they threw the cargo which was in the ship into the sea to lighten it for them. But Jonah had gone below into the hold of the ship, lain down and fallen sound asleep (v. 5).

The sailors, probably Phoenicians, were religiously convicted. Phoenicia, known for its seafaring trade, was a hub for Baal worship. Some of the mariners may have cried out to Baal in this perilous circumstance. That they were willing to toss their cargo overboard to lessen the weight of the ship depicts the life-threatening danger they encountered. This act was to no avail; the Lord created this

---

[5] Charles L. Feinberg, *Jonah, Micah, and Nahum: The Major Messages of the Minor Prophets Series* (New York: American Board of Missions to the Jews, 1951), 15.

catastrophe. The sailors did not petition for the aid of the true and living God but were seeking—unknown to them in their religiosity—the assistance of false deities. Nonetheless, they made an invocation.

Jonah, though, in a peculiar manner, slept comfortably in the extreme rear of the innermost part, "hold of the ship," during this treacherous hurricane. In the context of this verse, the Hebrew word for "asleep" is *radam*, signifying a deep sleep consistent with Sisera's heavy sleep that produced his exhaustion (Judg. 4:21). *Radam* is tantamount to the Hebrew word *tardemah*, which means *deep sleep* or *sound sleep*, or the divine anesthesia to which the Lord subjected Adam and Abraham (Gen. 2:21; 15:12). Jonah may have been extremely fatigued, or divinely assisted in his immersed, partial consciousness. It is unknown. Nevertheless, he appeared to be unworried.

Jonah's cozy rest is in profound contrast with the relaxed sleep of Jesus: "stern…on a cushion" in the boat (Mark 4:38). Even though both of them were content in in their rest, Jesus was in a *bed sleep* (Greek *katheudo*). Both slept conveniently but with entirely different motives. As Jesus slept in the boat, He tested His disciples' faith during the fierce wind and waves. Jonah slept in the bottom of the ship to find calm in the midst of the storm as he rebelled against the Lord, however.

A notable observation in Jonah's dispassionate attitude is that he was tasked to announce repentance to gentiles in a foreign land but had no concern for the troubled sailors, who unknowingly sailed him away from his assigned destination. Each seaman "cried to his god," denoting an appeal, a humble prayer, an entreaty, an introductory cry, a petition, a supplication, or even a statement of distress to false gods. Just as Baal failed to respond to the false prophets on Mount Carmel (1 Kings 18:26-29), the gods of the heathen sailors did not answer their plea for help. Yet, Jonah, the only man aboard the ship who knew the true and living God and could earnestly pray on their behalf, slept during the ordeal. His uncommon disposition actually compounded their fear. In all likelihood, Jonah's selfishness stemmed from his sin of defiance to the Lord.

So the captain approached him and said, "How is it that you are sleeping? Get up, call on your god. Perhaps *your* god will be concerned about us so that we will not perish" (v. 6).

Aghast by Jonah's ability to sleep soundly during this horrific storm, the captain advocated that he call on Yahweh (his God). The false gods did not reply to the sailors' initial cry (v. 5). Conceivably, the Lord would express concern for the welfare of the mariners. The uncertain captain had nothing to lose by making this suggestion since his crew—at least for the moment—was on the verge of total disaster. The Lord is concerned for the sailors. He wants to save the Ninevites of Assyria, although the sailors are not Ninevites. Tribal sects or the ethnicity of gentiles have no variation with God. The God of the Hebrews is the God of the gentiles. Abraham—from whom the entire Jewish nation originates—was a gentile. The subtle and moral premise of this dire situation is that the Lord will manifest grace to the unbelieving sailors at the disobedience of his own prophet.

"Get up," the words the sea captain used, have the same meaning as "arise," or the first word the Lord used in the second verse. The Hebrew word for both is *qum*, which means to *stand up* or *arise and let us go*. The ship commander had to remind Jonah of his duty. Instead of praying to the Lord, he slept during imminent danger while knowing the perils that his gentile companions faced. Jonah's behavior illustrated a lack of compassion for his fellow gentiles, which was adversative to the character of the Lord whom he served. He represented the Lord with willful and deliberate inadequacy, which eventually brought trouble to these men. It is a commonality for even pagans to seek divine intervention when they encounter danger, which

Jonah purposefully avoided. In fact, he did not care if he died. As a result, his comfy sleep.

The Lord's grand aim is to see a nation of gentiles come to repentance. But, in the interim, an ancillary—yet pertinent—lesson regarding gentiles is being taught to Jonah. In the New Testament, Jesus indicates that gentiles exhibited great faith (Matt. 15:21-28), and even more so than anyone in Israel (Matt. 8:5-10). The gentile captain displayed far more faith than Jonah did. Such action should have been reversed. "It is well known how often sin brings insensibility with it also. What a shame that the prophet of God had to be called to pray by a heathen."[6]

Each man said to his mate, "Come, let us cast lots so we may learn on whose account this calamity *has struck* us." So they cast lots and the lot fell on Jonah (v. 7).

Apparently, it was customary for heathens to cast lots to determine who was responsible for a catastrophic event (John 19:24). In the land of Israel, casting lots was a divinely prescribed methodical system of ascertaining the Lord's will (Lev. 16:8-10; Num. 33:54). Saul chose this process when he did not receive a direct response from the Lord (1 Sam. 14:36-42). Although it was performed by pagans, casting lots was a credulous practice. In this particular instance, the Lord nullified any perceived misconceptions the sailors may have had and furnished them with the true answer to their petition (Prov. 16:33). Whatever method they used, Jonah won the lottery. In the New Testament, the apostles cast lots to determine who would replace Judas Iscariot (Acts 1:26).

Then they said to him, "Tell us, now! On whose account *has* this calamity *struck* us? What is your occupation? And where do you come from? What is your country? From what people are you?" (v. 8).

---

[6] Ibid., 16.

Having believed what the Lord just revealed, the sailors identified Jonah as the perpetrator and demanded the full scope of this calamitous event. The shipmen proceeded to interrogate him by questioning his profession, place of origin, and ethnicity. They tried to determine if any of these factors might have contributed to their great trouble at sea. After all, Jonah was the only soul who was undisturbed by the storm. Presumably anxious, and with the ship at near destruction, the sailors had to identify a cause for this dire situation to provide a resolution to calm the sea.

He said to them, "I am a Hebrew, and I fear the LORD God of heaven who made the sea and the dry land" (v. 9).

"Hebrew" is the term by which the Israelites identified with their neighbors (1 Sam. 4:6, 9; 14:11). For this reason, it was an appropriate response, not to mention that Jonah boarded the ship in Joppa, which was a major port in Israel. Jonah's Hebrew ethnicity was probably a preamble to the explanation of his servitude to Yahweh Elohim, the "God of heaven who made the sea and the dry land." The Phoenicians referred to Baal as the sky god (cf. 1 Kings 18:24). The God who "made the sea and the dry land" by which the sailors traveled may have convinced them that Jonah had done a serious deed that warranted detrimental consequences. The Lord sought after him, and the sailors knew it. Another moral subtlety is that what was so obvious to the sailors was ambiguous to Jonah. When the Lord sovereignly elects someone into service to perform a specific task, that person cannot run away or hide from Him, which could prolong the mission, subject the servant to the Lord's discipline, and even hinder maturity or progressive sanctification. By his own admission, the prophet feared "the LORD God" and, with this confession, Jonah should have known that any attempt to flee from the Lord would be senseless. He had acquired nothing from this lesson.

Then the men became extremely frightened and they said to him, "How could you do this?" For the men knew that he was fleeing from the presence of the LORD, because he had told them (v. 10).

The sailors were frightened because they knew that the true and living God caused this extreme storm due to Jonah's disobedience. The exclamatory question of "how could you do this?" constituted the sailors expressing their disbelief of Jonah's ingenuousness in making a sea voyage to run away from the Lord, who created the sea. Jonah must have recognized that his deliberate disobedience would have consequential effects on the seamen. Evidently, he had previously told the sailors that he was "fleeing from…the LORD" (v. 3 states "from the presence of the LORD" twice). Prior to the great trouble, the sailors did not comprehend that God was the Creator of the sea. If the sailors had known Jonah's identity and initial intentions, they may not have sold him passage.

The interesting irony is that Jonah evidently denied God's sovereignty when he tried to escape His presence and elude his commissioned assignment. Also, even more paradoxically, the shipmen—now with a revelation of the God of the sea—were able to discern the Lord's response to Jonah's credibility. Surely, Jonah realized that, despite his best efforts, he could not evade the Lord. Thus far, Jonah had demonstrated juvenile defiance of the Lord and tranquil selfishness toward the sailors. Again, there appears to be a corrective lesson looming for Jonah in the Lord's objective of a projected Ninevite rebirth. (See comments about v. 6.)

So they said to him, "What should we do to you that the sea may become calm for us?"—for the sea was becoming increasingly stormy (v. 11).

With increasing tidal waves and high winds, the unsettled sailors resorted to Jonah for a solution. He knew how to placate his God's anger to reverse this misfortune. The sailors did not have a relationship with Yahweh. Hence, they—though experiencing momentary discernment of the Lord's bestowed revelation as a result of casting lots—could not provide resolution to quell the storm. So, they inquired of Jonah about what they should do with him to calm the sea.

He said to them, "Pick me up and throw me into the sea. Then the sea will become calm for you, for I know that on account of me this great storm *has come* upon you" (v. 12).

Jonah replied by telling them that throwing him in the sea would calm the storm because this storm was a result of his actions (or inaction). Jonah sincerely believed that the Lord would relax the waters if he terminated his flight from Him. The sailors—unaware of the insightful relationship between the Lord and His prophet—were probably extremely perplexed and apprehensive about Jonah's response. In their unpleasant experience, they faced undesirable options: if they took Jonah at his word, the sailors would hurl him in the sea at his request to save their own lives. However, if they did not toss Jonah overboard, the storm would not only continue but intensify, and their lives, in all likelihood, would not be spared. Additionally, there was minimal time to decide. Leslie Allen comments on Jonah's guilt:

> The piety of the seamen has evidently banished his nonchalant indifference and touched his conscience. By now he has realized how terrible is the sin that has provoked this terrible storm. The only way to appease the tempest of Yahweh's wrath is to abandon himself to it as just deserts for his sin. His willingness to die is an indication that he realizes his guilt before God.[7]

---

[7] Leslie C. Allen, *The Books of Joel, Obadiah, Jonah, and Micah: The New International Commentary on the Old Testament Series* (Grand Rapids: Eerdmans Publishing, 1976), 210-11.

Moreover, Jonah determined to die by electing to be thrown in the sea. If this occurred, the Lord's will for Nineveh would be voided. From an apparent christological perspective, Jonah was willingly prepared to perish, so the heathens could survive. He was willing to die in their place. At the outset, Jonah's rationale for his decision to die does not correspond to Jesus dying on the cross for the sin of mankind, though. Christ voluntarily set Himself apart for God's will (John 17:19) and fulfilled it (John 19:30). The Lord set Jonah apart to "cry against" Nineveh, yet he fled in the opposite direction. The decision to die, so that the sailors might live, developed from his reluctance to do the Lord's will. Once dead, Jonah would have certainly negated any opportunity for God to recommission him. Operation Nineveh? How would Nineveh have had a chance to repent if the prophetic messenger refused to come to the city, traveled in the opposite direction, caused a great storm because of his disobedience, and elected to die?

Compared to Christ with the condition of choosing to die sacrificially, Jonah is an enigmatic figure. The symbolism is surface at best. The work of Jesus is different in context. Christ's sacrifice resulted from unconditional love, selflessness, and obedience. Jonah's sacrifice was derived from hatred, selfishness, and disobedience, though Jonah's circumstances could be construed as the only conceivable option for the survival of the sailors. It can be argued that Jonah was also noble in a sense that his potential death would not merely save gentile sailors but Israel, as well. Jonah loved his country and, if he did not deliver a message of repentance to Nineveh, Israel— at least in his mind—would be secure from an Assyrian onslaught. Assyria was a prominent, rising world power destined to destroy Israel (Isa. 7:17; Hos. 9:3; 10:6-7; 11:5; Amos 5:27). This contention is without merit because the Lord designated Jonah to "cry against" Nineveh, which was the Lord's will. Although Assyria was a threat to Israel, the nation's safety and well-being were in the Lord's hands—not those of Jonah. God established Israel, and He would ensure its protection and guardianship (Ps. 121:4-7). It was the Lord's responsibility. Jonah certainly knew this.

However, the men rowed *desperately* to return to land but they could not, for the sea was becoming *even* stormier against them (v. 13).

Initially, the sailors did not entertain Jonah's suggestion. The captain considered ways to maneuver and navigate through the strong wind, back to Joppa, to drop him off. The thought of killing the Lord's servant was not a viable option. Their refusal to follow Jonah's advice could have reflected "a fear for his God and some concern for human life—even more than Jonah had for Nineveh."[8] Seeing that the Lord caused the storm and Jonah's self-willed wrongheadedness, it is indeterminable what the Lord would have done if the sailors put Jonah to death by hurling him into the sea. The sailors' respect for the Lord's prophet seemed grander than what Israel displayed for prophets at certain times (Matt. 23:34-36).

They fiercely tried to make their way back to land but were unable to do so. The storm climactically escalated; their efforts were futile. As time passed, the storm intensified in stages (1:4,11,13). Sensibly, the sailors reconsidered Jonah's proposal. With his offer potentially back on the table, as the storm strengthened, their dilemma tormented them.

Then they called on the LORD and said, "We earnestly pray, O LORD, do not let us perish on account of this man's life and do not put innocent blood on us; for You, O LORD, have done as You have pleased" (v. 14).

---

[8] Thrasher, "Jonah," 1364.

The sailors "called" or cried (Hebrew *qara*, meaning to *call* or *cry*) out to the Lord to assert their belief in God's sovereignty, which Jonah denied by his obstinacy. They acknowledged the Lord of the land and sea and requested vindication from any guilt for deciding to accept Jonah's offer. It seemed that no other recourse existed. In this instance, the pagan sailors totally relied on the true God to whom they were introduced. They may have just added the Lord to their god collection. No evidence exists that the sailors rejected their old gods.

In spite of that, a logical summation of the facts may have led the sailors to call on the Lord. First of all, the Lord caused the storm to emerge because of Jonah's disobedience. Second, while asleep below deck, Jonah was the only one at peace during this frightening experience. Third, to determine this great disaster, the sailors cast lots in which Jonah won the prize, which indicated the Lord was involved. Fourth, Jonah identified himself, announced the God he served, and explained to the sailors that he was the culprit who prompted the storm. To calm the storm, he advised them to cast him into the sea—to their reasonable apprehension. Lastly, the sailors cried out to the Lord and prayed to Him for mercy for the distressing decision they were about to make.

So they picked up Jonah, threw him into the sea, and the sea stopped its raging (v. 15).

Jonah was correct (v. 12). The sailors exercised faith in Yahweh and prevailed. The abrupt end of the violent waters proved to the sailors that the Lord truly controlled the sea (Matt. 8:26). Concerning his Ninevite mission, Jonah was being disciplined for his sin and faithless action.

Then the men feared the LORD greatly, and they offered a sacrifice to the LORD and made vows (v. 16).

The sailors' triumphant faith in God instituted a reverential fear of Him, as opposed to their initial frightening terror. They were afraid of the storm but were informed about its cause. For this reason, they feared the Lord. That the sailors offered a sacrifice and made vows to God indicates that Jonah may have told the sailors more about the Lord than what Scripture actually records. An ostensibly enigmatic, disobedient prophet displayed compassion to idol-worshiping, gentile mariners.

Sacrificial offerings and vows were not of supernatural origin. In fact, while sanctifying the Israelite nation in Leviticus (spiritually removing Israel from Egypt, i.e., sanctification of the nation), the Lord instructed the people about how to bring offerings and taught the priests how to make sacrifices to Him (Lev. 1-7). He instructed Israel how to handle vows under the Mosaic law, as well (Lev. 27). More than likely—due to the nature of the sailors' ominous circumstance—they did not have a full scope of these ordinances and precepts of the Lord. These particular elements were designated for the Israelites. However, by making a sacrifice and vows to the Lord, the sailors expressed sincere thankfulness and gratitude for delivering them from the torrential storm. This may have been their conversion, which fact is undetermined. Jonah's antipathy amounts to the Lord's manifested grace to a group of heathen sailors, yet the Lord targeted His grace to a larger gentile group, despite Jonah's insubordination. Ironically, the sailors feared and respected the Lord more than Jonah did.

Chisholm and Baldwin remark on the sailors' recognition of the Lord as a result of Jonah's defiance:

> In this episode the sailors are a foil for Jonah. In contrast to Jonah, who preaches but does not pray, the sailors offer prayers to God. In contrast to Jonah, who says he fears God but acts in a way that is inconsistent

with his claim, the sailors, who barely know Jonah's God, respond to him in genuine fear.[9]

Through the defection of Jonah a ship's crew acknowledges the Creator's power, comes to the point of worshiping him, and acknowledges him as Lord. If this is the outcome of Jonah's disobedience, what will God bring to pass as the result of Jonah's obedience?[10]

And the LORD appointed a great fish to swallow Jonah, and Jonah was in the stomach of the fish three days and three nights (v. 17).

At the inception, it seems unnatural for a fish to swallow a man. If a fish swallows a man, the odds are that the "great fish," at a minimum, will kill, possibly consume, or even regurgitate him. But the verse reads that "the LORD appointed a great fish to swallow Jonah." The species of the aquatic animal is unknown; however, the Lord can supernaturally assign a "great fish" of His specification to do His will. The belly of the fish housed Jonah for three days and three nights—emblematic of the time Jesus was in the heart of the earth after His crucifixion (Matt. 12:40). Although Christ was dead for only two nights, Hebrew reckoning is three days and three nights.

Regarding Jonah, there are two pertinent issues: Initially, the Lord performed a great miracle by preserving his life. He was not dead but held in the stomach of the "fish" for a brief time, though long enough. Under these circumstances, Jonah's natural survivability rate would have been zero. Second, although Jonah disappointed the Lord, He did not readily expel him of his mission. Even though Jonah resolved

---

[9] Robert Chisholm, *Handbook on the Prophets* (Grand Rapids: Baker Book House, 2002), 411.

[10] Joyce Baldwin, "Jonah," in *The Minor Prophets: An Exegetical and Expositional Commentary*, 3 vols., ed. Thomas Edward McComiskey (Grand Rapids: Baker Books, 1998), 2:563-64.

to die—and, in this era, he may have been considered as an aberrant deviant—he was still useful to the Lord. One's usefulness to God brings about a blessing. God delivered and restored Jonah as a conduit of liberation for a gentile nation, which was under His judgment for its sinful monstrosities. Similarly, and more significantly, God raised Jesus to life, so that He would be the instrument to offer an even greater salvation to the entire world that was additionally under His judgment for its sins. As far as the element of being detained in a "great fish" for three days and three nights, Jonah's release was an incidental precursor of Jesus's work, which required three days and three nights.

Many skeptics doubt the Lord's supernatural means to sustain Jonah's life in the belly of a "fish," but so many people "have been looking so hard at the great fish that they have failed to see the great God."[11] Nothing is impossible with the Lord (Luke 1:37).

---

[11] G. Campbell Morgan, *The Minor Prophets* (Westwood, NJ: Fleming H. Revell, 1960), 69.

CHAPTER 2

Then Jonah prayed to the LORD his God from the stomach of the fish, (v. 1)

The scene shifts from the storm and the sailors to Jonah and the fish. When thrown overboard, Jonah expected to die. But when he woke up inside the fish, realizing he was still alive, he recognized the goodness and graciousness of the Lord. Jonah may have perceived his rescue as the Lord's *extreme* mercy. The Lord extricated Jonah, despite his efforts to willingly die by drowning in an attempt to thwart the Lord's will. He saved Jonah from slow digestion, which was something Jonah had not anticipated, either.

Previously, the sailors asked Jonah to pray ("call on your God" [1:6]), but he prayed of his own volition this time. Unlike the shipmen, Jonah prayed to the Lord his God as a prayer of repentance. As the Prodigal Son, in a parable, repented and returned to his father (Luke 15:11-24), Jonah repented in prayer and in essence returned to his spiritual father, the Lord his God.

Prior to valuing the Lord's forgiveness, Jonah demonstrated nobility by sacrificing himself for the sailors and the preservation of

Israel—or at least from his perspective. But his commission does not call *his will* into question or into action. Jonah's objective was solely predicated on the Lord's will. He did not decide whether the nation of Israel would be protected or destroyed. The Lord's thoughts and ways are always above ours and Jonah's as the heavens are above the earth (Isa. 55:8-9). Knowing his dreadful situation, experiencing the inside of "the fish" (if he could even rationalize what it was), and understanding that God was graciously saving him, Jonah—by acknowledging his sin and with no other recourse at his disposal—prayed to the Lord.

The Frequency of Jonah's Prayer (vv. 2-9)

Jonah's prayer consisted of three elements: thanksgiving, contrition, and rededication. He began his prayer with words of *thanksgiving* toward the Lord (2:2-6). Though he cried out for "help" (v. 2), Jonah was already being rescued. Even when he was inside the fish, the Lord sustained his life (v. 6). As Jonah was being liberated, he expressed *contrition* (vv. 7-8), his sincere penitence, and remorse to God. He remembered the Lord (v. 7), and reproved and reprimanded himself for his own self-willed subterfuge (v. 8). After revealing true gratitude and displaying a heart of repentance, Jonah consecrated himself to the *rededication* of the Lord's will (v. 9).

and he said, "I called out of my distress to the LORD, and He answered me. I cried for help from the depth of Sheol; You heard my voice (v. 2).

Like many others, Jonah, in his stressful situation, called out to the Lord to seek "help." The Lord answered His servant's cry with deliverance (Pss. 3:4; 120:1). The latter part of the verse is a corresponding reaffirmation of the first part with a cry, instead of a call. Jonah "called" (Hebrew *qara*, meaning *summoned*) out to the Lord and "cried" (Hebrew *shava*, meaning to *cry for help*) for assistance. He first beckoned the Lord before he petitioned His aid. Because of Jonah's sin, he may have reasoned it appropriate to command the Lord's attention before he announced an emergency invocation. In any event, if an individual is extremely distressed and cries out to the Lord, it is highly unfathomable that He would not respond. In any case, the Lord already knows one's circumstance beforehand. In Jonah's case, He replied.

Jonah's cry "from the depth of Sheol" is analogous to "the stomach of the fish" (2:1). He associated the abdomen of the "great fish" (1:17) with an unescapable burial chamber. According to the Old Testament, Sheol is a habitation place—under the earth's surface—for unrighteous, wicked people. This is the home for those departed souls. The King James Version (KJV) commonly translates Sheol as *hell*. Jonah may have thought he had gone there to join the unrighteous dead (Ps. 18:4-5), but the Lord heard his voice.

"For You had cast me into the deep, into the heart of the seas, and the current engulfed me. All Your breakers and billows passed over me (v. 3).

Jonah realized that the Lord disciplined him by arranging the sequence of events surrounding the sailors' difficult decision to cast him into the sea to alleviate their physical and emotional stress as a result of the storm. "Into the heart of the seas" is symbolic to the sons of Korah who, in a song, invoked the Lord to be saved from death that arose from their affliction of the low pit and the depth of the dark places that rolled like waves of the sea (Ps. 88:7-8). Before he was swallowed by the fish, the waves or breakers submerged Jonah in billows, a heap of stone, or a rock garden. These effects overpowered him. Jonah accredited this action to the Lord.

Comparison in Psalms

Deliver me from the mire and do not let me sink; may I be delivered from my foes and from the deep waters (Ps. 69:14).

In this verse, David, who was deep in anguish, sought the Lord's deliverance from his enemies. Equivalently, Jonah knew that the sea breakers and billows belonged to the Lord. The highlight and dependence are on Him. In separate capacities, both David and Jonah were immersed in despair and desired the Lord's assistance. David agonized mentally; Jonah suffered physically and mentally.

Deep calls to deep at the sound of your waterfalls; all Your breakers and Your waves have rolled over me (Ps. 42:7).

Searching for the Lord in a time of trouble, the psalmist related his conditions to the cascading waves or breakers under a waterfall and compared the sound of the waves to the dangers that overwhelmed him. The breakers devastated Jonah, too.

"So I said, 'I have been expelled from Your sight. Nevertheless I will look again toward Your holy temple' (v. 4).

By his own admission, Jonah presumed the Lord removed him from His presence and thus forfeited his prophetic office. In a totality of unfavorable events, Jonah abandoned his commission by attempting to flee from the Lord; he caused a great storm to come upon gentile sailors in a ship; he—because he endeavored to abscond—nearly caused the ship to break apart, potentially killing the sailors; and he was on the verge of drowning by virtue of his own *professedly* selfish feat. So, in his estimation, Jonah assumed the Lord "expelled" him from His "sight," or turned away from him. David felt cut off from the Lord, as well, though he cried out to Him (Ps. 31:22). Still,

Jonah would "look again" to God's "holy temple" (synonymous with praying). The temple in Jerusalem is the place of prayer in Israel. In his prayer, Jonah knew that "salvation is from the Lord" (2:9); that is, only the Lord could save him. The Lord was his sole recourse. Jonah's prayer is indicative of humble gratitude, with an expression of thanksgiving to the Lord. Hearing and receiving Jonah's prayer, the Lord has not renounced him. "He felt he was cast out from the special regard and care which God exercises over His own. Now he realized how dire a thing it is to be apart from the presence of the Lord."[12]

Psalm Comparison

In my distress I called upon the LORD, and cried to my God for help; He heard my voice out of His temple, and my cry for help before Him came into His ears (Ps. 18:6).

When David was distraught about being pursued by his foes and Saul, David called upon the Lord for aid. From His holy temple, David's cry was attentive to the Lord's ears, and the Lord—with a supernatural invading thunderstorm—rescued David from his enemies. It is inconceivable that the Lord would not deliver Jonah in his present situation. In addition, his lament reached the Lord's ears. A declaration of emancipation for Nineveh was still in view, but Jonah (like David [by comparison]) sought the Lord's comfort, relief, and total reliance. The book of Jonah accentuates more than a rescue of foreigners. The prospective spiritual healing for Assyria was paramount; yet we should not undermine the Lord's work in Jonah in light of his assignment.

"Water encompassed me to the point of death. The great deep engulfed me, weeds were wrapped around my head (v. 5).

---

[12] Feinberg, *Jonah, Micah, and Nahum*, 25.

Submerged in the deep water, Jonah was on the precipice of drowning with marine algae covering his head. With hope obscured and death imminent, he appealed to the Lord (2:4).

Psalm Comparison

Save me, O God, for the waters have threatened my life. I have sunk in deep mire, and there is no foothold; I have come into deep waters, and a flood overflows me (Ps. 69:1-2).

As earlier indicated in Jonah 2:3 in contrast to Psalm 69:14, David's anxiety and acute mental suffering prompted him to request emancipation from his enemies (Ps. 69:14). The first two verses of this same psalm is David's initial plea to the Lord in the same analogy with aquatic illustrations, indicating that the hazard is a waterfall of sudden death to which he had plummeted, devoid of viable traction. David's single dependency is on the Lord. Verse 14 is David's nonverbatim reiteration of verses 1 and 2 of the same psalm. Just the Lord can save him. Equally, only the Lord could rescue Jonah, whose circumstances were more physically alarming.

"I descended to the roots of the mountains. The earth with its bars was around me forever, but You have brought up my life from the pit, O LORD my God (v. 6).

Jonah descended into the very foundation of the sea. He felt like an inescapable prisoner from physical death. Human aid seemed hopeless. Yet, the Lord elevated him from the threshold of Sheol (Pss. 49:15; 56:13; 103:4). Since Jonah fled from the Lord, his journey resulted in a constant *downward* helix. He traveled down to Joppa, down into the cargo hold of the ship, and down to the bottom of the sea near the gates of Sheol. "When you turn your back on God, the only direction you can go is down."[13] Jonah's ascendency would not occur until he returned to the Lord, as he prayed to Yahweh and displayed both adoration and penitence.

Psalm Comparison

The LORD will command His lovingkindness in the daytime; and His song will be with me in the night, a prayer to the God of my life (Ps. 42:8).

After comparing his afflictions to the sound of the cascading waves (Jon. 2:3 [Ps. 42:7]), the psalmist, nonetheless, will experience the Lord's love and lift up his voice in praise of Him day and night. The Lord will remain faithful to the psalmist and Jonah, providing both of them with twenty-four-hour protection (Ps. 121:6) for His "lovingkindness is everlasting" (Ps. 136).

"While I was fainting away, I remembered the LORD, and my prayer came to You, into Your holy temple (v. 7).

As Jonah envisioned his life nearing its end, he turned to the Lord. Though a distance from God, his prayer reached Yahweh in His heavenly abode. Even when David was in the cave to hide from his adversaries, who sought after his life, he cried out to the Lord and gave thanks (Ps. 142:5-7). David not only looked to the Lord as needed protection from the wicked, but indicated that he will enter God's dwelling place in the third heaven and bow in reverence to Him (Ps. 5:7). Faced with the likelihood of imminent death, both David and Jonah desired refuge in the Lord.

"Those who regard vain idols forsake their faithfulness, (v. 8)

---

[13] Wiersbe, *The Bible Exposition Commentary*, 381.

Jonah either philosophized or reflected on vain idols (empty vanities), which he had temporarily substituted in place of Yahweh. The Lord was his true love. Jonah's rational or empty vanities—or as they were deemed important to him (i.e., Israel's preservation)—superseded the Lord's will. Faithfulness to self amounts to faithlessness in the Lord. Jonah deserted his faithfulness to the Lord but returned to Him. Faith in human wisdom, apart from the Lord, is foolish vanity (Eccles. 2:14-16). Vain idol worship is a commonality among pagans and not a sanctioned practice for God's chosen nation, albeit it has occurred within the nation of Israel throughout Old Testament history.

"But I will sacrifice to You with the voice of thanksgiving. That which I have vowed I will pay. Salvation is from the LORD" (v. 9).

A sensible Jonah now rededicated his life to the Lord. Jonah was providentially hindered from presenting an animal sacrifice or a vegetable offering, so he made a sacrificial offering "with the voice of thanksgiving." This vow is an expression of faith and total recommitment to the Lord, from whom he departed but now has returned (Pss. 50:14; 107:22). "Salvation is from the Lord" is Jonah's summation and final word of his prayer as the ultimate assertion of his redevotion to Yahweh. Ironically, the Lord's salvation for Nineveh is what "fills Jonah with intense anger in the final chapter of the book."[14] The Lord will save Jonah and whomever He wills, even a gentile nation with a reputation for extreme barbarity.

Then the LORD commanded the fish, and it vomited Jonah up onto the dry land (v. 10).

---

[14] T. D. Alexander, "Jonah," in *Obadiah, Jonah, and Micah: The Tyndale Old Testament Commentaries Series* (Downers Grove, IL: InterVarsity Press, 1988), 118.

Prior to this verse, the Lord has performed five miracles—the hurling of a great wind on the sea (1:4), Jonah's lottery (1:7), the stillness of the raging sea (1:15), the appointment of a "great fish" (1:17), and the "great fish" that swallowed Jonah alive (1:17)—in this book. He will enact five additional ones before its conclusion. However, this sixth miracle, for many centuries, has perplexed many critics. Some contend that the fish vomiting "Jonah up onto the dry land" is simply narrative fiction. Just as the Lord made the stars and knows them by name (Gen. 1:16; Ps. 147:4; Isa. 40:26), though, He created the animals (Gen. 1:20-21, 24-25) and commanded them what to say (Num. 22:28-30) and do (Jon. 1:17; 2:10).

Moreover, Jonah glorified God by ascribing the miracle of this imposing aquatic creature to Him. That Jonah turned to the Lord during His preview of Sheol may have eliminated his prodigal status. He then was prepared to go to Nineveh to fulfill his assigned mission and speak to the souls who were destined for the underworld of death.

Additionally, the events that happened in chapters one and two are akin to the Lord's dealings and interactions with Israel. The symbolism is readily apparent. During a span of numerous years, Israel engaged in idol worship and possessed carnal proclivities that led to spiritual apathy. The nation departed from the Lord, which resulted in dire despair and frequent gentile oppression. The nation would turn back to the Lord, and He would deliver Israel from its anguish and misery. Correspondingly, Jonah fled from the Lord, ended up in a disastrous circumstance, prayed to God, and the Lord saved him from the brink of death in a miraculous fashion.

J. Sidlow Baxter records M. de Parville, a scientific editor of the *Journal des Debats* of Paris, who unpretentiously gives credence to Jonah's fish experience as he investigated the story of a man who survived after a sperm whale swallowed him:

In February 1891, the whale-ship *Star of the East* was in the vicinity of the Falkland Islands, and the lookout sighted a large sperm whale three miles away. Two boats were lowered, and in a short time one of the harpooners was enabled to spear the fish. The second boat attacked the whale, but was upset by a lash of its tail, and the men thrown into the sea, one being drowned, the other, James Bartley, having disappeared, could not be found. The whale was killed, and in a few hours the great body was lying by the ship's side, and the crew busy with the axes and the spades removing the blubber. They worked all day and part of all night. Next day they attacked some tackle to the stomach, which was hoisted on the deck. The sailors were startled by the spasmodic signs of life, and inside was found the missing sailor, doubled up and unconscious. He was laid on the deck and treated to a bath of seawater which soon revived him; but his mind was not clear, and he was placed in the captain's quarters, where he remained two weeks a raving lunatic. He was kindly and carefully treated by the captain, and the officers of the ship, and gradually gained possession of his senses. At the end of the third week he had entirely recovered from the shock, and resumed his duties.

During his sojourn in the whale's stomach Bartley's skin, where exposed to the action of the gastric juice, underwent a striking change. His face, neck, and hands were bleached to a deadly whiteness, and took on the appearance of parchment. Bartley affirms that he would probably have lived inside his house of flesh until he starved, for he lost his senses through fright and not lack of air.[15]

---

[15] J. Sidlow Baxter, *Explore the Book*, 6 vols. (Grand Rapids: Zondervan, 1966), 4:153.

Following this incident, it would be difficult for critics to disclaim Jonah's survival after being swallowed by a fish. James Bartley's experience is a proven fact, not fiction. As believers, we know Jonah's encounter with the "great fish" (1:17) to be true; we have the confirmatory Word from Christ Himself (Matt. 12:40). In essence, that resolves the speculation.

CHAPTER 3

Now the word of the LORD came to Jonah the second time, saying, (v. 1)

With the replacement of a few words— "now," and "second time"—as well as with the same grammatical order and the same syntactical address, Jonah 1:1 is reiterated. "Now," or at this juncture after the proceeding events happened, signifies the Lord has recommissioned him. A "second time" specifies the Lord twice has spoken this "word" (exact same "word" as in 1:1) to Jonah.

"Arise, go to Nineveh the great city and proclaim to it the proclamation which I am going to tell you" (v. 2).

This verse, like the previous one, repeats Jonah 1:2, with the exception of a few word changes. It affirms the same message. A loose, unconventional translation of this verse may express something like: *All right, Jonah....You fled, nearly sank, prayed, repented, and now have been emancipated from the belly of the fish. Let's try this again! Go to Nineveh, and proclaim my proclamation to the Ninevites!* Even in this uncustomary rendering of the text, the Lord is still sovereign over the storm, the fish, Jonah, and Nineveh. The Lord substantiates His solemnity in His second message to Jonah.

The "great city" (see notes on 1:2) of Nineveh was located approximately 550 miles northeast of Samaria, which was the capital of Israel during the divided kingdom. The Lord's sovereignty will be evidenced through the instructional, precise message that He will bestow on Jonah. By now, Jonah should have recognized that he is not an agent of his own conceptualization, predicated on his own personal feelings and emotional content, but a conduit of the Lord as a prophetic messenger called to disclose the Lord's words in concordance with His will.

So Jonah arose and went to Nineveh according to the word of the LORD. Now Nineveh was an exceedingly great city, a three days' walk (v. 3).

Jonah did as the Lord commanded him to do. Parenthetically, this was his first act of obedience. The Lord delivered Jonah from Sheol and would have protected him from any harm he may have feared because "God will never lead you where the grace of God can't keep you and the power of God can't use you."[16]

Interestingly enough, the Lord three times titles Nineveh as "the great city" (1:2; 3:2; 4:11). In this particular verse, He describes Nineveh as "exceedingly great." Great (Hebrew *gadol*) means *extremely* or *far more*, exactly as it states. No hidden meaning exists. The greatness of Nineveh refers to the size of the city.

Diodorus Siculus, who was a notable Sicilian historian and contemporary of Julius Caesar, asserted that Nineveh was a parallelogram. Its horizontal sides represent thirty-six miles, and the vertical sides denote twenty-four miles with a circumference of

---

[16] Wiersbe, *The Bible Exposition Commentary*, 383.

roughly sixty miles. In addition to its size, Nineveh, as indicated in **Assyrian Cruelty**, was a leading city of one of the most dominant nations in the world. Accordingly, the Lord said it was not only "great," but "exceedingly great," and a "three days' walk," which covers sixty miles—presumably, twenty miles a day. Based on Siculus's description of Nineveh's landscape, Jonah's feet may have hurt.

Then Jonah began to go through the city one day's walk; and he cried out and said, "Yet forty days and Nineveh will be overthrown" (v. 4).

Jonah arrived in Nineveh to commence his assignment. He possibly walked at least twenty miles, which can be computed as "one day's walk" through the city. The previous verse indicates it was a "three days' walk." Jonah may have walked for three days or less, but a "day's walk" is recorded and, through the course of his journey, he probably reverberated the forty-day overthrow of Nineveh. It is highly unlikely and seemingly improbable that, considering the distance traveled and all the people encountered, Jonah would have mentioned merely once the potential demise of Nineveh.

Note that Jonah's message was a broadcast of forthcoming judgment—not a call of salvation. Nations under prophetic doom that refuse to repent would, in fact, be destroyed (Jer. 18:7-8). If Nineveh repented, the city could evade judgment (Joel 2:12-14). For the Ninevites, this possible physical relief seemed more appealing than spiritual salvation did. In the New Testament, Jesus brought forth the gospel (good news), which was a message of hope. Believers of this message would be exonerated or justified from the penalty of sin of eternal damnation—thereby avoiding a spiritual, second death—and be declared righteous for repenting and accepting Jesus Christ as their Savior. By believing in Christ, Christians eliminate total depravity and complete spiritual destruction. In contrast, Nineveh, by believing the message of tragedy due to its inhumane carnages, would evade physical devastation and complete annihilation. With respect to the Lord's will and how He deals with certain individuals and specific nations in the dispensation of time throughout history, He brings a message of judgment and hope.

The forty-day timeline may refer to the reflective past of the rebellious, Egyptian-redeemed, first-generation Israelites when Moses instructed the people of the second generation (Deut. 9:23-25). Because the first generation refused to take possession of the land that the Lord gave them and did not obey his voice in the Lord's judgment, Moses "fell down before the Lord" (Deut. 9:25) for forty days and forty nights to prevent their destruction. However, their rebellion resulted in the Lord's judgment on them. They wandered in the wilderness for forty years and died, never having entered the promised land.

Respectively, Nineveh's wickedness—possibly compounded with the repudiation of the Lord's proclamation via Jonah—would result in its eradication, as well. Even so, Jonah's simple message contrasts with Nineveh's great might. God's Word is able to alter the hearts of the most contemptible and advanced gentile population.

Then the people of Nineveh believed in God; and they called a fast and put on sackcloth from the greatest to the least of them (v. 5).

It is uncertain whether Jonah traveled three days but, apparently after "one day's walk," the people responded to his message with repentance and "believed in God" (Yahweh). The repentance is factual and true; yet, it seems quite impractical that a gentile, polytheistic nation would become proselytes to Judaism in complete conversion to Jewish monotheism. The entire citizenry—from the nobles to the impoverished people—fasted and wore "sackcloth," which indicate a time of mourning, sorrow, and self-affliction that brought forth humility (2 Sam. 3:31,35; 1 Kings 21:27; Neh. 9:1-2; Isa. 15:3; 58:5; Dan. 9:3; Joel 1:13-14).

The fast of the Ninevites appears to be absolute, characterized by a complete abstinence from food and water (3:7) as in Acts 9:9—not to be confused with a normal fast (Luke 4:2), or a partial fast (Dan. 10:3). The Hebrew word *saq* ("sack") for "sackcloth" is a transliteration of the word, rather than a translation. Sackcloth, which was material made from camel or goat hair, was worn during a time of mourning, sorrow, or distress. Because of Jonah's warning (3:4), this action would be essential for the Ninevites.

Dubiously, would Nineveh concede to merely eight spoken words (3:4) from a foreign prophet without any variation of an amplified explanation? Did these people question who sanctioned the message? Who gave Jonah the authority to deliver such a message? Could the Ninevites have seized Jonah and put him to death in a treacherous, exhibitive manner as they did others? According to Warren Wiersbe (see citation 16), the Lord sovereignly protected Jonah in the land of the brutal gentiles. The Assyrians suffered earthquakes and famines and endured political rebellions in the early to mid-eighth century. These elements may have been construed as signs of divine judgment. Jonah's message may have added weight to their critical circumstance. He did "the Assyrians a favor and has gone to a great deal of trouble to do so. He has nothing to gain."[17] However doubtful critics may be, the best plausible explanation is that the Lord compelled Jonah.

Furthermore, Christians believe these events to be true because Christ Himself said so (Matt. 12:40-41; Luke 11:29-30). This is the ultimate empirical evidence of this text, with God delivering abominable gentiles, manifested as the christological purpose of the book of Jonah. After Israel rejected Jesus, He spoke in parables and

---

[17] John H. Walton, *Zondervan Illustrated Bible Backgrounds Commentary*, 5 vols. (Grand Rapids: Zondervan, 2009), 5:114.

eventually directed His ministry to the gentiles. He later called Paul—whose missionary journeys consisted of travels to various gentile regions—to bear His name before them (Acts 9:15).

When the word reached the king of Nineveh, he arose from the throne, laid aside his robe from him, covered *himself* with sackcloth and sat on the ashes (v. 6).

Since Nineveh was the leading and largest city in Assyria, the king of Nineveh might also have been the king of Assyria. Ahab and Ahaziah, kings of Israel in their respective reigns, were both labeled as the "king of Samaria" (1 Kings 21:1; 2 Kings 1:3). During Jonah's era, either Adad-nirari III (811-783 BC) or Shalmaneser IV (783-772 BC)—undetermined—reigned on the throne in Assyria. In any event, the pagan ruler humbled himself, traded his royal robe for sackcloth, and sat on an ash heap (Job 42:6; Isa. 58:5).

Knowledge of Jonah's encounter with the fish could have reached the king prior to his arrival in Nineveh. Possible gastric acid from the interior of the "great fish" (1:17) may have stained or bleached his skin and thereby substantiated his experience. A decolorization of Jonah's skin is practical speculation but plausibly true. Additionally, he traveled a great distance to deliver the Lord's message. With all these factors—feasible, previous familiarity with a miraculous event concerning a fish; possibly whitened skin of a Hebrew prophet as a result of this miracle; and a reluctant foreigner perceivably risked his life to cry against a pagan nation—the king of Assyria could not condone or undermine these factors. He responded in accordance with the Lord's will.

He issued a proclamation and it said, "In Nineveh by the decree of the king and his nobles: Do not let man, beast, herd, or flock taste a thing. Do not let them eat or drink water (v. 7).

This proclamation asserts the seriousness of the king and his nobles about their condition. In addition to exchanging his festal robe for sackcloth, the king decreed a citywide penitence in an absolute fast (cf. Acts 9:9) for all the living—man and animals. The animals needed no remorseful repentance (and they cannot do so), but their mandated participation in this fast disclosed their owners' spirit.

"But both man and beast must be covered with sackcloth; and let men call on God earnestly that each may turn from his wicked way and from the violence which is in his hands (v. 8).

The sackcloth covering extended to the animals. To decorate animals in the time of sorrow or mourning has been a standard commonality for some time.

The Ninevites associated their imminent judgment with their own repulsive behavior. The Lord was astutely aware of the atrocious violence that the Ninevites inflicted on others. Their cup of brutality was full. For this reason and considering they were warned, the notion of terminating their wickedness could incur the Lord's mercy and deter His wrath.

In Hebrew, violence (*chamas*) is a malicious wrong. Merriam-Webster defines violence as "the exertion of physical force so as to injure or abuse...as if by infringement or profanation."[18] Pertaining to the Assyrians, violence was the overbearing encroachment imposed on others to obtain power and control over them. Assyrian soldiers were extremely violent (Nah. 3:3) and dominated others through fierce conquests. Rabshakeh, an Assyrian official, arrogantly implied Assyria's seeming invincibility (2 Kings 18:33-35). In an early section of Genesis, violence inundated the entire world. Thereupon, God announced the destruction of the world and its violators (Gen. 6:11,13).

---

[18] *The Merriam-Webster Dictionary: New Edition* (Springfield, MA: Merriam-Webster Inc., 2004), 808.

Without a change in perspective, Nineveh may have suffered the same fate in an urban setting. The Noahic covenant prevented God from destroying the earth by water again (Gen. 9:11).

"Who knows, God may turn and relent and withdraw His burning anger so that we will not perish" (v. 9).

History claims that Nineveh was a polytheistic, pagan nation; yet, after they heard the Lord's message, the people "believed in God" (3:5). They believed in the true and living God (Yahweh) with a capital G—not the man-made, nonexistent gods (lowercase g) who denote pseudo-deity, fraudulent power, and fictitious authority in many gentile regions that highly esteemed them.

The Ninevites relied on Yahweh with uncertainty but, with a positive outlook, they thought that the Lord would yield and renounce His sweltering infuriation, so they would not "perish." But due to their ambiguity—despite hearing Jonah's message and in spite of fasting, wearing sackcloth, and humbling themselves before the Lord—the Ninevites had no complete assurance that the Lord would spare them. Hence, the words "who knows." The Lord's turning and relenting were derived from His compassion, which the Ninevites reckoned when they repented. Nineveh had not realized that its humbling actions went before the Lord. Jonah's witnessing was supposed to prevent the nation from perishing. The essence of spiritual salvation is "that whoever believes in Him shall not perish, but have eternal life" (John 3:16). The language in this book "is a challenge to all to hear God's appeal to be like the sailors and the Ninevites in their submissiveness to Yahweh."[19]

When God saw their deeds, that they turned from their wicked way, then God relented concerning the calamity which He had declared He would bring upon them. And He did not do *it* (v. 10).

---

[19] Allen, *The Books of Joel, Obadiah, Jonah, and Micah*, 189.

The Ninevites incurred God's pleasure when they repented. Consequently, He waived His declaration of "calamity." God's decision not to judge Nineveh was not a vacillatory act of His being. God does not waver but is consistent in His character. The Lord's response to Nineveh's obedience is germane to man's change of heart. It may have appeared that the Lord changed His mind, but His display of mercy to the repentance of man is one of His gracious attributes. The potter and the clay are illustrations in Jeremiah 18 that reveal the divine character of God.

Chapter 4

Though Jonah hardly comes across as a hero anywhere in the book, he appears especially selfish, petty, temperamental, and even downright foolish in chapter 4.[20]

But it greatly displeased Jonah and he became angry (v. 1).

The Lord's relenting of His judgment on Nineveh may have angered Jonah for two likely reasons. First of all, this, of course, means that Nineveh would avoid annihilation. Jonah—at least not in his day—would not see the "great city" crumble and fall. Although the people of Nineveh repented, the city was still a prominent, powerful, leading force surrounding the nations. Second, the Lord's mercy on Nineveh may have sown a seed in Jonah's mind that the pagan nation would eventually revert to its depravity and spread its might southwest to Israelite territory. Such would ultimately result in a dismal future for Israel. He may have foreseen simply a temporary—not a permanent—change in Nineveh. Jonah did not want the Assyrians to destroy Israel.

---

[20] Douglas Stuart, *Hosea-Jonah, Word Biblical Commentary Series* (Waco, TX: Word Books, 1987), 502.

Hence, the Lord's decision to extend merciful compassion to the Ninevites infuriated him considerably.

He prayed to the LORD and said, "Please LORD, was not this what I said while I was still in my *own* country? Therefore in order to forestall this I fled to Tarshish, for I knew that You are a gracious and compassionate God, slow to anger and abundant in lovingkindness, and one who relents concerning calamity (v. 2).

Jonah prayed to the Lord concerning His compassion, lovingkindness, and gracefulness. He knew that the Lord would not judge the Ninevites if they obeyed His command to repent. While in Israel, Jonah either spoke to the Lord about His forgiveness or talked with a fellow countryman regarding the Lord's kind hand. Either way, he prayed a dismal prayer of anger and frustration. Jonah sought a different outcome for Nineveh, which was most likely a bad arbitration contrived in his heart that was contrary to the Lord's will.

Textual evidence that involved the recent turn of events explains Jonah's psychological construction. To begin with, Jonah's second prayer to God is significantly different from his initial prayer (2:1-9). With the first prayer, he exhibited thankfulness, remorsefulness, and rededication toward the Lord. Though he opted to die by permitting the sailors to cast him into the sea, Jonah—while in the belly of the fish, which the Lord prescribed—cried out to God to be rescued from Sheol. So, initially he wanted to die but, evidently, while he teetered on the precipice of death, Jonah changed his mind. Nonetheless, the Lord, through His divine will, had already concocted a plan to save him, despite his willful defiance. Jonah knew the compassionate ways of the Lord, abandoned his assignment, desired to die, and prayed to the Lord with respect to his disobedience, all while being saved. He repented and was recommissioned. Since the Lord exercised mercy on Nineveh, Jonah prayed to the Lord and indicated the reason he fled in the first place—to hinder His forgiveness. He realized that the Lord would be "slow to anger and abundant in lovingkindness, and one who relents concerning calamity." After Jonah revitalized his relationship with the Lord (2:1-9), his feelings and emotions should have been consonant and not inconsistent with the Lord's will. He wanted Nineveh to be eradicated.

In an analysis of Jonah's evolving mental state, it appears that he was *stubbornly reluctant, mentally repentant, a perceivable vacillator, and needlessly frustrated*. When Jonah expressed to the Lord, "Was not this what I said while I was still in my own country?" it shows that he recognized the Lord would pardon the Ninevites based on their repentance. Prior to his journey, he may have speculated in his mind two likely scenarios: Nineveh would repent, and the Lord would withhold His wrath; or Nineveh would spurn Jonah's message, and the Lord would seal its doom. In this immaterial, hypothetical situation, Jonah factually conceded to the former. Accordingly, he was *stubbornly reluctant* to travel to Nineveh; and, by his own admission, he averted the mission.

Being enclosed in the stomach of a large, amphibious animal potentially covered in gastric acid is nothing one can possibly fathom, other than it is an unpleasant circumstance in which no one would like to be found. As Jonah descended deep into the sea and was rescued by the God-appointed fish, his heart and mind—once adamantly campaigning against the Lord's will—resorted to the sole One who could emancipate him. Jonah's authentic prayer (2:1-9) is not in dispute. However, even after the fish discharged him onto dry land—and though he was grateful, contrite, and recommitted to the Lord—Jonah was still adversely opposed to the Lord for not judging Nineveh. His first prayer was one of thanksgiving; his second prayer was one of anger. By implication, Jonah was double-minded. He thanked the

Lord for saving his life, but he had no interest in lost souls. For these reasons, Jonah was *mentally repentant* and a *perceivable vacillator*.

After Nineveh did exactly what Jonah had anticipated, in prayer, he expressed disdain: "Please LORD…in order to forestall this I fled to Tarshish." Jonah needed to learn that this is the Lord's story (His-story) and not his tale. God's election of Israel does not mean reduced or minimal love for the gentiles. His selection for the reprieve of Nineveh is not arbitrary. Jonah was the first Old Testament missionary to communicate conditional absolution to a gentile nation that the Lord deemed worthy of saving. Jonah had to see beyond his inconsequential will and look through the lens of the One who designated him for this task. As such, Jonah felt just the relevance of his own will. Consequently, he was *needlessly frustrated*. Jonah commended the Lord for His great qualities; only, he wished God was not so great. In summation, there is a stark "contrast between God's compassion (3:10) and Jonah's displeasure, and between God's turning *from* His anger (3:9-10) and Jonah's turning *to* anger."[21]

"Therefore now, O LORD, please take my life from me, for death is better to me than life" (v. 3).

Jonah's rage was so immense that he preferred "death" over "life." During their own individual vexation of different circumstances, Moses, Elijah, and Jeremiah expressed this same sentiment. The constant complaints of the Israelites and their demand for food heavily burdened Moses so much that he demanded that the Lord take his life (Num. 11:10-15). After revealing the grand power of the true and living God on Mount Carmel and slaying four hundred fifty false prophets of Baal (1 Kings 18:20-40), Elijah, in fear of Jezebel's threat to his life,

---

[21] John D. Hannah, "Jonah," in *The Bible Knowledge Commentary: Old Testament*, ed. John Walvoord and Roy Zuck (Wheaton, IL: Scripture Press Publications, Victor Books, 1985), 1470.

fled to the wilderness to die (1 Kings 19:1-4). Overwhelmed with the extreme persecution in Judah, Jeremiah cursed the day of his birth (Jer. 20:14-18).

All three of these servants were within the providential will of the Lord when they announced their desire to die. The motivation for death—not to say that desiring to die in general is good—for these prophets corresponded with the goodness of the Lord, though. Moses yearned for obedience; Elijah wanted a national revival; and Jeremiah desperately promoted repentance. Jonah craved the extermination of an entire pagan city. It was, of course, to no avail; but, unlike the three aforementioned prophets, Jonah's catalyst for death did not harmonize with the righteousness of the Lord. The goodness of the Lord disturbed Jonah to the point of depression.

The LORD said, "Do you have good reason to be angry?" (v. 4).

Knowing what He ordained beforehand and understanding Jonah's emotional fury about Nineveh's blessed outcome, the Lord asked Jonah if he reserved the right to be angry—particularly angry against Him for not administering judgment on a repentant nation that exercised faith in that He would "relent and withdraw His burning anger" (3:9). By His own sovereign will, the Lord will bestow grace, mercy, and compassion on whomever He desires (Exod. 33:19; Rom. 9:15). This was not Jonah's, but the Lord's divine prerogative. Because of the Lord's mercy, Jonah might fear the presumable future Assyrian oppression of Israel. Though a legitimate concern, this matter was not Jonah's affair. He does not decide who lives and who dies. Jonah is an instrument of designated communication, working in congruence with the Lord's divine plan. Jonah did not have a noble "reason to be angry."

Incidentally, the Lord's question to Jonah was not a rebuke but a challenge, suggesting that he could have considered the situation incorrectly. Jonah criticized the Lord for not being angry (4:2); the

Lord *gently* contested his frustration. Jonah's anger arose from not comprehending the Lord's action in light of His character as so many other servants did (e.g., Job, Habakkuk, Jeremiah, et al.). Divine tenderness prevails over human displeasure.

Then Jonah went out from the city and sat east of it. There he made a shelter for himself and sat under it in the shade until he could see what would happen in the city (v. 5).

Still bitter about the Lord's divine mercy, Jonah departed east to the city and sat under a self-constructed "shelter." The Hebrew word for shelter is *sukkah*, which is a *thicket*, a *booth,* or a *hut*. During the Feast of Tabernacles, the Israelites made these leafy structures (Lev. 23:40-42; Neh. 8:14-18). Jonah sat under this leafy vine perhaps to ascertain whether the Lord would change His mind and judge Nineveh. He would have to wait forty days.

Jonah's exasperation with the Lord's action or inaction prevented him from complete comprehension of his ministry and the Lord's blessing. His abandonment of the city proved that he assessed the situation from his own perspective. Like the elder brother in the parable of the prodigal son, he refused to enter and celebrate the feast (Luke 15:28). Likewise, Jonah declined to be in a city that he felt deserved eradication. Jonah served as a means to bless Nineveh but missed out on his own blessing by becoming considerably consumed with the preservation of Israel. His attitude should have been ingratiated and in sync with the Lord's will.

So the LORD God appointed a plant and it grew up over Jonah to be a shade over his head to deliver him from his discomfort. And Jonah was extremely happy about the plant (v. 6).

While waiting, the Lord "appointed a plant" to provide Jonah with shade from the sun (though the shelter shielded him, as well [4:5]) and to alleviate his "discomfort" (Hebrew *ra'ah*) from the oppressive heat. This leafy structure, probably considerable in size to offer such consolation, elated Jonah. The solace that the plant afforded is equivalent to the compassion and mercy the Lord bestowed on the Ninevites, thereby canceling the heat of judgment. The prevailing notion was that Nineveh could express gratitude toward God for His forgiveness. If the Lord could administer soothing satisfaction to His own incensed prophet, He could surely grant sympathy to malignant foreigners. The range of "God's mercy to the undeserving is the theme that continued to elude Jonah even as he experienced it."[22]

But God appointed a worm when dawn came the next day and it attacked the plant and it withered (v. 7).

By attacking the "plant," God's use of the worm would change Jonah's comfort to uneasiness. The "worm" is the Lord's introductory illustration of affliction to come, exemplary of what Nineveh would have received. This is the commencement of hypothetical judgment (not actual because the Lord already relinquished His judgment [3:10]) slated for Nineveh that erases all pleasurable contentment. This is Jonah's continued lesson from the first chapter initiated by the Lord for his initial disobedience. The strain on the Lord's sovereignty lingered. The Lord "appointed" (Hebrew *manah*, meaning to *appoint, provide,* or *prepare*) a storm to end Jonah's unauthorized journey; He *provided* a fish to save him from drowning; He *prepared* a plant to soothe Jonah despite his anger; and He *appointed* a worm to remove Jonah's comfort. The Lord obviously manipulated Jonah's circumstances to teach him a valuable lesson.

---

[22] *The Nelson Study Bible*, 1499.

When the sun came up God appointed a scorching east wind, and the sun beat down on Jonah's head so that he became faint and begged with *all* his soul to die, saying, "Death is better to me than life" (v. 8).

In addition to the withering plant that eliminated Jonah's shade, the Lord intensified his "discomfort" (4:6) by sending a sirocco—a dry, hot, oppressive, "scorching east wind." The powerful sirocco, added to the sweltering Middle-Eastern sun, compounded Jonah's agony to the point that he resolved to die a third time (1:12; 4:3, 8). The sovereign agents of the Lord would exclude any shelter for Jonah. He was beyond suffering since he experienced helplessness, hopelessness, and misery. These elements exemplified the previous lost state of Nineveh. Jonah endured the anguish he wished the Lord would have brought to Nineveh. The Lord delivered him from his self-initiated "calamity" (1:7-17; 2:1-10) only to have it return. Rather than discerning that the Lord treated him impartially and repenting of his attitudinal sin, Jonah became angrier and more depressed, and he demanded death.

Then God said to Jonah, "Do you have good reason to be angry about the plant?" And he said, "I have good reason to be angry, even to death" (v. 9).

The Lord was responsible for the death of the plant. In responding to the Lord's question, Jonah advised that he had just cause to be "angry about the plant." Unrighteous fury fed his ego and produced a selfish heart. Even after Jonah's fervent prayer to the Lord and following the manipulative sequences to which the Lord had subjected him, Jonah's heart was still not in compliance with His will.

In the first chapter, Jonah sinned against the Lord. In chapter two, he lamented for help; the Lord saved him; and he repented. In chapter three, Jonah traveled to Nineveh to preach the Lord's proclamation.

He yielded his mind but never his heart to the Lord's will. God's will, not Jonah's, was fulfilled. For this reason, Jonah desired to die, albeit he had no "good reason to be angry" (in response to the Lord's question [4:4]) since the Lord's will supersedes his will. Jonah's motivations were defectively prioritized. His anxiety for the plant is proof. "If Jonah could be concerned for a day-old plant and relief from his physical 'discomfort' then he should share the Lord's concern for the people of Nineveh and the terrible 'calamity' threatened against them."[23]

Douglas Stuart underscores the pinnacle of Jonah's acrimonious heart and God's compassion toward Nineveh:

> The double question in 4:4 and 4:9 . . . is unmistakably the key to the book's central message. The climax of the story comes here—not with the repentance of the Ninevites in chap. 3 or at any other point—when God challenges Jonah to recognize how wrong he has been in his bitter nationalism, and how right God has been to show compassion toward the plight of the Assyrians in Nineveh.[24]

The New Scofield Reference Bible compares Jonah's attitude to some contemporary Christians:

> In these last verses the great missionary lesson of the book is sharply drawn: Are the souls of men not worth as much as a gourd? Like Jonah, God's people today are often more concerned about the material benefits

---

[23] Al Fuhr and Gary Yates, *The Message of the Twelve: Hearing the Voice of the Minor Prophets* (Nashville: B&H Academic, 2016), 3216, Kindle.

[24] Stuart, *Hosea-Jonah*, 435.

so freely bestowed upon us by God than about the destiny of a lost world.[25]

Then the LORD said, "You had compassion on the plant for which you did not work and *which* you did not cause to grow, which came up overnight and perished overnight (v. 10).

Jonah's "compassion" (Hebrew c*hus,* meaning to have or show *pity*) for the "plant" that grew and expired "overnight" is akin to his appreciation for the Lord's love for Israel. Jonah did not deposit the "plant" or establish Israel; yet, he concerned himself with the "plant" and was indifferent to the Ninevites' fate. Jonah's contorted concern for the "plant," for which he did nothing, was immensely imbalanced with the Lord's concern for Nineveh that He rescued. The Lord expressed sympathy for the Ninevites; Jonah displayed positional apathy toward them. Plainly, Jonah's admiration for the Lord's love of Israel infused his life so much that it swarmed out any empathy for people who had no solid familiarity with, but were in need of a relationship with, Yahweh. If the Lord has pity on lost souls, His servants must share this same rapport. Farfetched as it may seem, Jonah, in the Lord, brought faith to a "great city" but did not feel love for Ninevites, to whom he preached. Jonah may have been oblivious to, or ignored, the fact that the Lord created the people of Nineveh and the plant. God reserves the right to do for each as He deems in accordance with His will.

"Should I not have compassion on Nineveh, the great city in which there are more than 120,000 persons who do not know the *difference* between their right and left hand, as well as many animals?" (v. 11).

---

[25] *The New Scofield Reference Bible*, ed. Frank E. Gaebelein, William Culbertson, et al. (New York: Oxford University Press, 1967), 942.

In conclusion, the Lord inquired of Jonah regarding his "compassion" for the city with "more than 120,000" individuals believed to be in mental infancy. These "who do not know the difference between their right and left hand" is a signification of the apparent children in the city. Children's inability to distinguish from their "right and left hand" may credibly refer to their moral illiteracy. Although responsible for their innumerable massacres and in peril of divine judgment, the people of Nineveh did not possess the benefit of a special divine revelation pertaining to the moral will of the Lord. They subscribed to and worshiped false gods so, ethically and morally speaking, they were like children in addition to the actual juveniles and infants in the region.

The reference to "animals," the final word in the book, is the conclusive climax to the Lord's lesson to Jonah, which extends to the Israelites and the church. According to the created order, animals fall under man's authority (Gen. 1:26). God created man in His own image (Gen. 1:27). If the Lord has "compassion" on "animals" (and He does), how much more should Jonah, the Lord's servant, experience sympathy for God's created beings, who are subjected to His judgment for their transgressions (3:8)? Douglas Stuart details the worth of animals as a basis for Jonah's nonargument for his anger:

> It is possible, of course, that the animals are mentioned because animals are *ipso facto* innocent and also lack intellectual prowess. Thereby Jonah and the audience would understand that the Ninevites, likewise, are innocent and stupid. But a more likely reason for the mention of animals is that they constitute the middle point in the worth scale upon which the argument of Yahweh is based. That is, the people of Nineveh are of enormous worth. They are human beings, and they are the citizens of the most important city of their day. The animals in turn are of less worth, but still significant in

the economy of any nation or city.... The gourd, on the other hand, is of minor worth.... Jonah has furiously argued for the worth of a one-day-old plant (v. 9). He can have no good argument, then, against the worth of Nineveh, with all its people and animals.[26]

Regardless of circumstances or how one feels about a particular sect of people, the salvific message of hope must extend to those who contest Christians. Our concern for the safety of the saints, as in Jonah's concern for the welfare of Israel, must not prevent the Lord's will from moving forward. The Lord, as He did for Jonah, will provide a hedge of protection over us.

The Lord begins the book with a commandment (1:2) and concludes with a question posed to Jonah, whose response is undetermined. Prayerfully, he responded with grace and gratitude and realized the lesson the Lord taught him was in concert with saving Nineveh. Nevertheless, God, the ultimate author of Jonah ("All Scripture is inspired by God" [2 Tim. 3:16]), has the final Word, and His sovereignty will always prevail over His human intermediary servants who oppose it.

---

[26] Stuart, *Hosea-Jonah*, 508.

NAHUM

Author and Background

Little is known about the prophet Nahum, whose name means "comfort," "consolation," or "compassion," other than that he was an Elkoshite from the town of Elkosh. The exact location of this town has yet to be ascertained. Elkosh may have been Nahum's birthplace or his place of ministry. No one knows, except that he was a Jewish prophet. It is conjectured that El-Kauzeh, an ancient area that the tribe of Naphtali occupied, is a modern extension of the undiscoverable Elkosh. Some scholars propose that Elkosh was situated in the vicinity of Galilee, near Capernaum (City of Nahum, Kaphar-Nahum, or the Village of Nahum). Others suggest that Nahum lived somewhere in Judah or east of the Jordan River. In a speculative analysis, when Samaria or the ten tribes of Israel fell to the Assyrians in 722 BC, Nahum and others may have been deported to Mesopotamia. Nahum may have managed to return to Judah sometime later. He addressed Judah (1:13,15), and readers may insinuate that he wrote from Judah. Additionally, this may explain why Nahum is acquainted with Assyrian affairs.

DATE

The Assyrian king Ashurbanipal conquered the Egyptian city of No-amon, which is also known as Thebes, in approximately 663 BC. Because Nahum referenced this defeat (3:8-10), he apparently wrote after such occurrence. He foretold the fall of Nineveh, which took place in 612 BC. Nahum's prophetic timeline probably fell between 663 and 612 BC. Thus, his ministry should have occurred during the reigns of Manasseh (696-641 BC), Amon (641-639 BC), and Josiah (639-608 BC).

PURPOSE

Nahum's communication is twofold: He prophesied an oracle of judgment *to* the Neo- Assyrian Empire and its capital, Nineveh. The message was *for* the Jews, though. Like Obadiah and Jonah, Nahum's prophecy was a note to the nations. "Nahum's prophecy was the complement to Jonah, for whereas Jonah celebrated God's mercy, Nahum marked the relentless march of the judgment of God against all sinners world-wide."[27]

Nahum disclosed that the Lord would obliterate Nineveh as a retribution for the Assyrians' viciousness to various nations, including the Northern Kingdom of Israel, in 722 BC. In addition to conquering the Northern Kingdom, Assyria decimated many Judean cities and ineffectively besieged Jerusalem in 701 BC. The remaining Judeans in the land, who resided under Assyria's silhouette, were vulnerable to this ferocious onslaught. Hence, Nahum's book constitutes a proclamation of Nineveh's fall, therein providing solace and encouragement to the Judeans with confidence that the Lord is completely sovereign. He is the "just governor of the nations who

---

[27] Walter C. Kaiser Jr., *Toward an Old Testament Theology* (Grand Rapids: Zondervan Publishing House, 1978), 221.

will punish wicked Nineveh and restore His own people."[28] Although God selected Assyria to act as a catalyst of punishment against a recalcitrant and obstinate Israel (Isa. 7:17; 10:5-6), "he holds that nation corporately responsible for the excesses and atrocities committed in fulfilling this role (Isa. 10:7-19; Zep. 2:14-15)."[29]

CHARACTERISTICS

Nahum's forty-seven-verse prophecy is not assembled in an anthology (such as Micah), nor is it a narrative (like Jonah), yet it is an oracle of judgment written in well-poetic, delineated literary form with tremendous rhetorical skill. He uses imagery and literary rhetoric to employ a considerable variety of metaphors to convey his message. Nahum's rapid staccato lines of poetry denote a perception of imminent chaos and pandemonium in the visions of Nineveh's eradication. He boldly and actively taunts God's adversaries, while mastering allusion with the application of symbols of Assyria to magnify their merited justice. These literary features alone distinguish Nahum from other prophets. The Lord guided Nahum to construct the body of the prophecy into a chiastic (reverse word order, diagonally arranged) structure:

> A. Assyrian king taunted/Judah urged to celebrate (1:2-15)
>   B. Dramatic call to alarm (2:1-10)
>   C. Taunt (2:11-12)
>   D. Announcement of judgment (2:13)
>   E. Woe oracle (3:1-4)
>   D. Announcement of judgment (3:5-7)

---

[28] Richard D. Patterson, *Nahum, Habakkuk, Zephaniah: Wycliffe Exegetical Commentary Series* (Chicago: Moody Press, 1991), 53.

[29] David W. Baker, *Nahum, Habakkuk, and Zephaniah: An Introduction and Commentary*, *The Tyndale Old Testament Commentaries Series* (Downers Grove, IL: InterVarsity Press, 1988), 23.

C. Taunt (3:8-13)

B. Dramatic call to alarm (3:14-17)

A. Assyrian king taunted as others celebrate (3:18-19)[30]

THEOLOGICAL THEME

Nahum is sequential to the book of Jonah, who prophesied during the previous century. Unlike Jonah—who declared the Lord's absolution of Nineveh—Nahum tells and describes the future execution of the Lord's judgment. Just as God will bless those who bless His covenant people, in the same breath, He will bring retribution on those who defy His law (1:8, 14; 3:5-7) and afflict His elected nation (Gen. 12:3). God possesses punitive judgment against evil, which is also redemptive, loving, and encouraging to the faithful—namely, Judah—whose existence Nineveh threatened.

God's judgment on Nineveh is a twofold—Godward and manward—necessity. First of all, there is a sin of pride against God. Sennacherib's invasion of Jerusalem (Isa. 36) represented pride in rebellion against God's sovereign rule over His creation. This sin was a gargantuan one of Nineveh. Next, the city exhibited immeasurable savagery toward its fellow men—which was yet another substantial sin. The Assyrians were notorious for their oppressive malignancy to other people. The sins of pride (Godward) and cruelty (manward) are intertwined together so much. When there is pride against God, typically, cruelty exists toward other people. Jesus imparted that the two greatest commandments are to love God wholeheartedly and love our neighbors as ourselves (Matt. 22:37-39). Incidentally, these two commandments summarize the ten commands—with the first commandment encapsulating the first four (Godward, Exod. 20:3-4, 7-8), and the second commandment outlining the last six (manward, Exod. 20:12-17). When individuals exercise them, they are not proud

---

[30] Chisholm, *Handbook on the Prophets*, 428.

and cruel. Pride and cruelty are completely contrary to the will of God. Consequently, He pronounced judgment on Nineveh to punish its pridefulness and to protect the people.

Nahum states that "an overflowing flood" would completely end Nineveh (1:8), and the city would be hidden (3:11). The Babylonians entered the city as the overflow of the Tigris River demolished many city walls, and, following Nineveh's complete devastation in 612 BC, the site was not unearthed until 1842. Assyrian pride and cruelty were buried forever.

NOTABLE THEME

Retribution is the motif. The Lord avenges His enemies.

KEY VERSES

A jealous and avenging God is the LORD; the LORD is avenging and wrathful. The LORD exercises vengeance on His adversaries, and He reserves wrath for His enemies (1:2).

The LORD is good and a stronghold in the day of trouble, and He knows those who take refuge in Him (1:7).

OUTLINE

I.   The Oracle (1:1)
II.   Nineveh's Doom Proclaimed (1:2-14)
    A. The Lord's anger and goodness (1:2-8)
    B. The Lord's provisions for Nineveh and Judah (1:9-14)
        1. The Lord speaks to the consumption of Nineveh (1:9-11)
        2. The Lord encourages and emancipates Judah (1:12-13)
        3. The Lord speaks to the extermination of Nineveh (1:14)

III. Nineveh's Calamity Detailed and Justified (1:15-3:19)
  A. The Lord's sovereign justice to Judah and Israel (1:15-2:2)
  B. The descriptions of and reasons for Nineveh's destruction (2:3-3:19)
  1. Invaders advance on Nineveh (2:3-7)
  2. Invaders capture the city and taunt their captives (2:8-13)
  3. Nineveh's merciless bloodshed and idolatry (3:1-7)
  4. Nineveh's vanity and self-confidence (3:8-19)

SUMMARY

Nahum, who identifies himself as the author (1:1), conducted his prophetic ministry during the reigns of Manasseh, Amon, and Josiah, who were kings of Judah (2 Kings 21-22). God purposed Nahum with an oracle of judgment on Nineveh for plotting evil against the Lord (1:11) and, more specifically, oppressing Israel and Judah. The paramount theme of Nahum's book is God's vengeful retribution.

When Jonah reluctantly preached a message of repentance to Nineveh slightly more than a century earlier, the Ninevites repented of their wickedness. As a result, the Lord spared His judgment on the ruthless gentile nation, much to Jonah's dismay. As time passed, the message of repentance—to the subsequent Assyrian generations—may have not been communicated. If imparted, the message was possibly ignored; or, if received, it was later revoked (see **Preface**). In 722 BC, the Assyrians destroyed the Northern Kingdom. They scattered the Israelites into other territories and occupied their land. With Israel out the way, Judah was in Nineveh's view. The Lord prohibited the Ninevites from demolishing Judah. In keeping with the Abrahamic covenant, God will not tolerate tyrannical oppression of His people, and iniquity will not go unpunished (Gen. 12:3). Nahum's message of the Lord's oracle of judgment is underscored in three chapters:

the declaration of judgment on Nineveh (1), the detailed description of Nineveh's judgment (2), and God's rationale for Nineveh's judgment (3).

Nahum's oracle marks a reverse course from Jonah's proclamation. Since Jonah wanted to witness Nineveh's eradication, he surely would have marveled with respect to Nahum's words. Nineveh's sinfulness had run its course. The Lord vindicated His holiness on this brutal, pagan nation when three gentile associations (see **Preface**) annihilated the city of Nineveh, which delineated the conclusion of the Assyrian Empire. God illustrated to the world that "might does not, in the long run, make right, and that even the mightiest infidel is absolutely helpless before the judicial wrath of Yahweh. This invincible empire, so successfully maintained, toppled in ruins never to arise again."[31]

---

[31] Gleason L. Archer, *A Survey of Old Testament Introduction* (Chicago: Moody Publishers, 2007), 335.

EXPOSITION

CHAPTER 1

The oracle of Nineveh. The book of the vision of Nahum the Elkoshite (v. 1).

Nahum introduced this book as an "oracle" of prophecy to Nineveh. An "oracle" is a message from the Lord, which typically pronounces judgment. It can be burdensome because it regularly contained a message that lay heavy on the prophet's heart and was delivered and interpreted as a weighty message of devastation. Nahum was the sole messenger who proclaimed a divine "oracle" of doom on Nineveh.

A jealous and avenging God is the LORD; the LORD is avenging and wrathful. The LORD takes vengeance on His adversaries, and He reserves wrath for His enemies (v. 2).

Three paramount words in this verse relate to the character of the Lord: jealousy, "vengeance," and "wrath." Jealousy is the envious desire to possess what one has. It is essentially the intolerance of rivals. It also is treasuring what one owns and wanting to justifiably protect it.

In the latter instance, jealousy is virtuous. Depending on the validity of the rival, jealousy can be a virtue or a sin.

Since the Lord created all things and everything, He envies no person; however, He is the one true God who is jealous with regard to His glory, honor, and all that belongs to Him. He desires to share them with no tormentor of His sovereign elect. He is God alone. Nahum painted the Lord as the jealous One of His chosen people (Exod. 20:5; 34:14; Deut. 4:24; 5:9) and as immensely concerned about their welfare (Num. 25:11; Deut. 6:15). Nineveh's malevolent treatment of Israel and Judah stimulated the Lord's jealousy and provoked Him to vengeance.

Scripture generally portrays vengeance as a sin. For one to retaliate against an individual, or a group of people, for an unjust, egregious action is not consistent with the law of the Lord. He alone possesses vengeance and retribution. He will bestow justice on all His adversaries and all who hate Him (Deut. 32:35, 41). The Lord's people prayed to Him to avenge their enemies when they attacked them. The people of God acknowledge that vengeance is His when they sought His support (Ps. 94:1-2). The Lord's vengeful action to judge the unrighteous, who oppress His people, is the virtue of jealousy indicated in His character and in keeping with His promise in the Abrahamic covenant (Gen. 12:3).

The Lord's wrath is the determinative, suitable penalty designated for His "enemies." "Wrath" (Hebrew *hemah*), which means *to be hot,* depicts the torrid rage and austere fury that allude to the Lord's anger. In this verse, the Lord's fury was rationalized in the principal root of Nahum's prophecy. The following verses, which lead to the book's conclusion, reveal the righteousness and the fervent ardor of the Lord applied on behalf of His people. Nineveh's cup of iniquity was full, and the Lord's reserved "wrath" would pour down on the Ninevites' cup like a torrential hurricane, with no avenue of escape and nowhere for their atrocity to travel.

The LORD is slow to anger and great in power, and the LORD will by no means leave *the guilty* unpunished. In whirlwind and storm is His way, and clouds are the dust beneath His feet (v. 3).

Patience, which is a fruit of the Spirit (Gal. 5:22), is the long-suffering the Lord endured to exhale His righteous "anger." He did not operate in haste; rather, the Lord "is slow to anger" (Exod. 34:6; Num. 14:18), which exudes the peak of a boiling point. "Outbursts of anger" constitute a sin of the flesh (Gal. 5:20), but this deed is the culmination of making provisions for the flesh as applied to the believer. An eruption of fury due to carnal actions is not righteous anger; it is sin. There is a distinction between sinful anger and righteous anger. The Lord's anger, of course, is the latter. He waited long enough to render His judgment on Nineveh.

The Lord's "great…power" is suitable with His measured "anger." The Assyrians abused the Israelites for an extended period of time long after the Lord spared Nineveh at the message of Jonah. That the Lord has prodigious supremacy makes the prospect of God releasing His anger petrifying (Deut. 8:17-20). No "guilty" person will fly under the Lord's radar. It is impossible. His sensors encompass the entire earth. His judgment is not always swift—as in the case of the devil and fallen angelic host (Matt. 25:41)—but it is certain.

The "whirlwind," "storm," and "clouds" are metaphoric descriptions that underscore the exasperated aspect of the Lord's character and power as it relates to Assyria's punishment. Literal whirlwinds and storms can cause extensive property and structural damage, which result in an insurmountable calamity. The rhetorical use of these words is equivalent to the Lord's "anger," which He will exhibit to Nineveh. The Lord is so grandiose that the "clouds" in the atmospheric, first heaven are for Him as the "dust" on the ground is for humans (2 Sam. 22:10; Ps. 18:9). The "clouds" above are akin to "dust" particles to God, who resides in the third heaven.

He rebukes the sea and makes it dry; He dries up all the rivers. Bashan and Carmel wither; the blossoms of Lebanon wither (v. 4).

Descriptions of the Lord's power are indicated in His ability to dry up the "sea" and the "rivers" with simply a spoken word. The Lord's power in speech is implied; He demonstrated this ability in creation (Gen. 1). More specifically, if the Lord can direct the waters to be grouped into one location with the appearance of dry land (Gen. 1:9), He can retract the "sea" and "rivers," as well. The Lord manifested this power when He parted the Red Sea (Exod. 14:21). The psalmist even attests to this event (Ps. 74:13). Additionally, Yahweh prohibited the Jordan River from flowing, so the Israelites could cross on dry ground (Josh. 3:16-17).

Even the opulent regions of "Bashan," "Carmel," and "Lebanon" could weaken and "wither" at the Lord's utterance. Physical heat causes bodies of water to dry up and land to wane or diminish, but the spiritual heat of the Lord's wrath in judgment can be the facilitator for physical heat. Physical and spiritual heat can be synonymous.

Mountains quake because of Him and the hills dissolve; indeed the earth is upheaved by His presence, the world and all the inhabitants in it (v. 5).

"Mountains" are the most solid, unmovable, topographic features on earth, though Mount Sinai "quaked violently" when "the Lord descended upon it in fire" (Exod. 19:18). This ability was merely a minute exhibition of His majestic power. If the Lord can make the mountains collapse, the slightly less unstable "hills" would surely tumble at His command. His "presence" can cause the entire "earth" to include every occupant to upheave (Hebrew *nasah*, meaning to *lift*) and tremble (Heb. 12:18-21). Hence, the Assyrian Empire would not be an arduous task for the Lord to depose.

In Mark 11:23, when addressing His disciples, Jesus said, "Truly I say to you, whoever says to this mountain, 'Be taken up and cast into the sea,' and does not doubt in his heart, but believes that what he says is going to happen, it will be *granted* to him." This metaphor is a typical one in Jewish literature for rabbis or spiritual leaders, who were charged to solve seemingly irresolvable problems. Contextually, this verse instructs the believer to trust in the Lord's unlimited, awesome power, so that one will see how mightily He works. The Lord can literally move stable, physical mountains, along with constant, spiritual afflictions or recurrent, extreme difficulties that are analogous to actual mountains. Again, as indicated in the fourth verse, physical aspects can parallel the spiritual realm.

Who can stand before His indignation? Who can endure the burning of His anger? His wrath is poured out like fire and the rocks are broken up by Him (v. 6).

Nahum uses two rhetorical questions to highlight the Lord's enraged "anger." The Hebrew translation for the word indignant is *zaam*, which means to *abhor* or to *become enraged*. To be enraged is equivalent to scorching-hot water that boils over. No one can withstand God's unimpeded wrath. In these two rhetorical inquiries, both the questioner and the questioned know the answer, or at least presume to recognize the answer. The Lord's "wrath" is discharged "like fire," which spreads throughout an entire region and even causes pieces of rock to break up (1 Kings 19:11). The Assyrians might have contemplated their pending judgment and the somberness of the Lord, considering He obliterated their entire army as it encircled Jerusalem in a single night (2 Kings 18:13-19:35). If the Lord's wrath can be poured out like fire and break up "rocks," flesh, blood, and man-made erected edifices will not stand a chance against "His anger."

The LORD is good, a stronghold in the day of trouble, and He knows those who take refuge in Him (v. 7).

God is virtuous in a beneficial, delightful, and favorable way. The term "good" is a well-known attribute of the Lord, who reverberates throughout Scripture. All who believe know that "the Lord is good" (Ps. 100:5). God's people will benefit from relief from the fear of being conquered by a repugnant, pagan nation. Any concerns they may have maintained about encountering the Assyrians in battle after Nahum's declaration oracle were erased. The people of God delighted in the Lord's decision to remove the Assyrians from existence. Judea would no longer entertain future threats or hostile conflicts from the overconfident, arrogant heathens. The Lord's people have favor with Him because He elected the Jewish nation in Genesis, too. They are His chosen people (Gen. 12:1-3). The Lord is the sanctuary for His people, whom He will rescue in the "day of trouble" (Ps. 50:15).

By comparison, the Lord is not only noble in anger but vengefulness (Rom. 11:22). No hill, mountain, physical sanctuary, or a great entrenched city like Nineveh can provide better security than safety in Him, particularly when people encounter anxiety or angst (Pss. 27:1; 37:39). Moreover, "He knows" and draws near "those" who place their complete confidence, trust, and "refuge in Him." This verse is a momentary shift from the Lord's impending dealings with the Assyrians to the encouragement and faith of the Israelites.

"The Lord is good" connotatively: His righteous anger is revealed in His decision to administer judgment on Nineveh. Yet, Nahum promulgates His asylum for the Israelites in their day of distress. The Lord's nobility equates with a certain doom and a sure, safe haven. In both instances, His righteousness prevails.

But with an overflowing flood He will make a complete end of its site, and will pursue His enemies into darkness (v. 8).

In this verse, Nahum makes two literal assertions and perhaps two metaphorical connotations. He begins by swinging the pendulum back to the emphasis of his oracle—the wrathful aspect of the Lord's character. The brief attention to the Lord's people, without the use of their name in the prior verse, exemplifies His expressed attributes toward them.

The "overflowing flood" could be the destruction of Nineveh—as some traditions have claimed—in conjunction with the flooding of the Tigris River in 612 BC. Alternatively, Nahum emblematically describes the Lord's total and permanent eradication of Nineveh as "He will make a complete end of its site." Darkness is literally night after sunset. Yahweh could "pursue His enemies into darkness" from daylight and kill them as they attempt to flee His terror. They would not evade the Lord because of the passage of time within the day. It may have taken all night, but it is certainly not a laborious task for Yahweh. Because fighting was so problematic at night, battles typically ceased at nightfall and resumed at daybreak. This could have been an actual and realistic occurrence; or Nahum referred to "darkness" as a symbol of evil—what Nineveh exhibited—and eternal judgment—what Nineveh deserves (Job 17:13; Prov. 4:19; Isa. 8:22; 42:7; Matt. 8:12; John 3:19; Col. 1:13; Jude 6).

Whatever you devise against the LORD, He will make a complete end of it. Distress will not rise up twice (v. 9).

Not any well-concocted plan of extreme intellectual prowess will be enough to frustrate or thwart the will of God. He can and will eliminate any such strategy that is contrived against Him. Twice distressed refers to Sennacherib's initial besiegement of Jerusalem as king of Assyria (2 Kings 18:13). It never happened again. The Assyrians, who opposed the Lord's people, were actually in opposition to the Lord Himself. After Nineveh collapsed in ashes, it was never reestablished. The Lord made "a complete end of it."

Like tangled thorns, and like those who are drunken with their drink, they are consumed as stubble completely withered (v. 10).

Though they are tough to unhook or unwrap, "tangled thorns" cannot withstand fire. The bristles will be breached. Correspondingly, the consternation of the Ninevites—as when their city was under attack—is even more compounded by their "drunken" (Hebrew *saba*, meaning to *drink heavily* or *heavy drinkers*) stupor. They were inebriated. As follows, the Lord would destroy the entire Assyrian nation as easily as the angel of the Lord struck down 185,000 Assyrians in one night (2 Kings 19:35).

From you has gone forth one who plotted evil against the LORD, a wicked counselor (v. 11).

This "one" may refer to Sennacherib, the Assyrian king, "who plotted evil against the Lord" and opposed Him (2 Kings 18). The wicked king's vicious scheme will have severe repercussions on the entire nation of Assyria.

Thus says the LORD, "Though they are at full *strength* and likewise many, even so, they will be cut off and pass away. Though I have afflicted you, I will afflict you no longer (v. 12).

Nahum temporarily shifts from Nineveh to highlight Judah.

"Thus says the Lord" indicates that what Yahweh declares will happen with absolute certainty. Even though the Assyrians are strong and plentiful, the Lord will obliterate them. They will "be cut off" from existence and "pass away" from antiquity.

The Lord had "afflicted" the Israelites with Assyrian dominance but not anymore. He would afflict them "no longer." God's people may have been perplexed by this proclamation because Israel had feared

Assyria for centuries. The latter part of the Lord's announcement, "I will afflict you no longer," is the precise statement that Israelites will be liberated only from Assyrian affliction since other nations did trouble them after the Lord removed Assyria from the scene.

"So now, I will break his yoke bar from upon you, and I will tear off your shackles" (v. 13).

The Lord breaking the Assyrian "yoke bar" and tearing "off… shackles" from the Israelites is analogous to releasing the yoke from an ox's neck and shattering a prisoner's chain link. God will emancipate His people from an endured Assyrian oppression—namely, invasion, besiegement, and inhabitation (2 Kings 19:20-37; 2 Chron. 32:1-23; Isa. 37:27-38).

The LORD has issued a command concerning you: "Your name will no longer be perpetuated. I will cut off idol and image from the house of your gods. I will prepare your grave, for you are contemptible" (v. 14).

The prophet reverts God's message back to Nineveh.

Neither Nineveh's "name," nor its kings' names, will be preserved. The population, to include the king, will have no surviving descendants. Their existence will cease. No future offspring of the king will surface numerous years later to create an edict of destruction for the Lord's people like that of Haman the Agagite, a descendant of King Agag—the ruler of the Amalekites, whom King Saul destroyed, but captured and spared the king (1 Sam. 15:2-9). Saul's failure will not be replicated in this decree. The Babylonian coalition will not overlook any Assyrian.

The Lord pledged to destroy the idols of Nineveh and remove them from their temples. Ironically, the Assyrians frequently carried away the idols of nations they conquered to manifest the supremacy of their gods over those they subjugated, as did the Philistines when they defeated Israel in battle and carried away the ark of God (1 Sam. 4:10-11). "The conquering Medes, however, despised idolatry and did away with multitudes of images that existed in Nineveh."[32]

The Lord will metaphorically and literally arrange the tomb for the "contemptible," disgraceful city of Nineveh. He will figuratively bury Nineveh by designating others to demolish it. In addition to being destroyed, the city will be factually concealed until archaeologists, by digging trenches in Kuyunjik (ancient Nineveh), paved the way for Assyriology in 1842.

Behold, on the mountains the feet of him who brings good news, who announces peace! Celebrate your feasts, O Judah; pay your vows. For never again will the wicked one pass through you; he is cut off completely (v. 15).

Someone traveling over the mountains with a message of "good news" and "peace" constitutes the imagery of tranquility and not anxiety. Future deliverance from oppression is imminent; hence, Judah is urged to "celebrate" and live righteously in the expectation of the Lord's coming deliverance. The Lord answered their prayers. As a result, Judah should "pay" its "vows" to Him. The Assyrians will never "pass through" Judah's land ever again. The pagan nation, as in metaphorical scissors, "is cut off completely" like a piece of clothing that is forever separated from the entire garment. Such as the attire, there are no reattachments; like Nineveh, there will be no future recurrent threats to Judah. Incidentally, Nahum spoke as though Nineveh had already crumbled, and the messenger had recently arrived with a good report.

---

[32] Feinberg, *Jonah, Micah, and Nahum*, 132.

Chapter 2

The one who scatters has come up against you. Man the fortress, watch the road; strengthen your back, summon all *your* strength (v. 1).

The king of Nineveh is disparaged and scoffed in the first chapter. In verses 1 through 10 of the second chapter, the Lord sends the city a stressful alarm call.

"The one who scatters" is the Lord, who will scatter Nineveh in destruction. He is their frightening and awesome opponent, whom they will not overcome. The Assyrians are "up against" a triple collaboration of human warriors, who are a product of God's will. So, in essence, Nineveh is not contending with the Medes, the Babylonians, and the Scythians, but with the Lord. The four commandments— "man the fortress" (or stand on the fortress wall); "watch the road" (be vigilant of the roads leading to the city); "strengthen your back" (stand strong, or don armor); and "summon all your strength" (be courageous or dauntless)—are sarcastic taunts to the Ninevites concerning their futile efforts to defend themselves against the Lord's wrath and avoid defeat.

For the LORD will restore the splendor of Jacob like the splendor of Israel, even though devastators have devastated them and destroyed their vine branches (v. 2).

Returning to Judah again, Nahum underscores the restoration of Judah—perhaps like the former united kingdom ("like the splendor of Israel") in contrast to the destruction of Nineveh. Nineveh, which experienced prosperity and great joy, would undergo immense destruction; whereas Israel, which suffered colossal devastation, would become magnificent again. The plural usage of the pronouns "them" and "their" indicates that both Judah and Israel (the former Northern Kingdom) will experience splendid exaltation in the millennial kingdom established by Christ, the Messiah. The unique irony is that "devastators" (Assyrians) will become the "devastated." It is extremely probable that the conquering Assyrians "destroyed" many of Israel's literal grapevines; however, "vine branches" represent the Israelites, too (Ps. 80:8-16; Isa. 5:1-7).

The shields of his mighty men are *colored* red, the warriors are dressed in scarlet, the chariots are *enveloped* in flashing steel when he is prepared *to march,* and the cypress *spears* are brandished (v. 3).

The prophet—who speaks in the present tense, possibly to capture the graphic nature in which the Lord will ravage Nineveh—directs his attention back to the Lord. The invading "warriors" possessed "red shields" and wore red uniforms, a known color favorite of the Babylonians and the Median armies (Ezek. 23:14). The red could have been splattered blood on the soldiers carrying shields, or it could be the color from the copper that covered both shields and uniforms. The enclosed, surrounding "chariots" with blades or "flashing steel" that protruded from their wheels, along with their wielded "spears," demonstrated their readiness for battle.

> These images speak of blood, violence, and warfare. Isaiah refers to the custom the Assyrians had of rolling their outer garments in blood before a battle (see Is. 9:5) to strike terror in the hearts of their opponents. Here the tables would be turned. While others would have 'shields,' 'chariots,' and 'spears,' the people of Nineveh would be bathed in blood—their own blood.[33]

The chariots race madly in the streets, they rush wildly in the squares, their appearance is like torches, they dash to and fro like lightning flashes (v. 4).

Because of the invaders' dashing pursuit through Nineveh's "streets" and "squares," the "chariots," which formed a daunting war machine, would appear to be luminous "torches," bolting "to and fro" proportionate to "lightning flashes." The proficiency of the charioteers influences the imagery of this verse.

He remembers his nobles; they stumble in their march, they hurry to her wall, and the mantelet is set up (v. 5).

The Assyrian king called upon his military and community leaders to resist the onslaught of the attackers and defend the city of Nineveh, but their confusion and perplexity are synonymous with one stumbling in haste to take action. They scurried to their seemingly safeguarded walls only to encounter a large, defensive, portable shield ("mantelet") established by the attackers to deflect arrows and stones, which occurs when an army besieges a city.

The gates of the rivers are opened and the palace is dissolved (v. 6).

---

[33] *The Nelson Study Bible*, 1516.

The fall of Nineveh is presumed to be associated with the besiegers, who entered the city through its flooded waterways. The attack came at a time when the flooding from the "rivers" destabilized the wall and the defense of the city, which thereby caused destruction to the "palace." The Tigris River, along with two of its tributaries—the Khosr and the Tebiltu—streamed near Nineveh's walls and essentially passed through the city. Nearly all Nineveh's fifteen gates contained water passage from either of these streams.

> Diodorus wrote that in the third year of the siege heavy rains caused a nearby river to flood part of the city and break part of the walls.... Xenophon referred to terrifying thunder (presumably with a storm) associated with the city's capture.[34]

It is fixed: She is stripped, she is carried away, and her handmaids are moaning like the sound of doves, beating on their breasts (v. 7).

Nineveh's future is "fixed," meaning that its defeat has been determined with unequivocal assurance. The city is "stripped" of all its possessions and "carried away" into captivity or other domains. The servant girls of the lower social economic scale, along with the distinguished nobles, will lament over the destruction of the city. Their mournful cry would sound like a dove's coo and the flapping of its wings ("beating on their breasts").

Though Nineveh *was* like a pool of water throughout her days, now they are fleeing; "Stop, stop," but no one turns back (v. 8).

Nineveh was a reservoir of goods and assets from other nations it conquered. The city and its population were overpowered with an

---

[34] Elliott E. Johnson, "Obadiah," in *The Bible Knowledge Commentary: Old Testament*, 1495.

imminent, colossal defeat they could not elude. Everyone turned a deaf ear to their panic as the people shouted, "Stop, stop." The nation with such pride in the specialization of taking others captive would not be taken captive by others. The Assyrians reap what they sowed (Hos. 8:7; Gal. 6:7).

Plunder the silver! Plunder the gold! For there is no limit to the treasure—wealth from every kind of desirable object (v. 9).

Through centuries of great conquests, trading, and taxation, Nineveh had amassed immense wealth. In fact, it was the wealthiest historic city in the Near East during the seventh century BC. Now what the Ninevites had done to others would be reciprocated to them. "Plunder the silver! Plunder the gold!" This phrase was the exclamation of no limitation to the treasures the invaders would acquire at Nineveh's expense.

> According to historical records, the Medes were the first to breach the defenses of Nineveh. Later, the Babylonians successfully attacked it. The Medes, however, were not interested in a long-term occupation of the area, but in a quick profit.[35]

She is emptied! Yes, she is desolate and waste! Hearts are melting and knees knocking! Also anguish is in the whole body and all their faces are grown pale! (v. 10).

The invaders cleared out all Nineveh's treasures. The city was deflated and existed in a deserted, uninhabitable barren state—an essential garbage dump. The people of the once strong and robust city observed their destruction and were flattened with fading hearts,

---

[35] Tremper Longman III, "Nahum," in *The Minor Prophets: An Exegetical and Expositional Commentary*, 2:807.

knocking knees, and psychological sorrow throughout their entire bodies, accompanied by pale faces, which provided them their own personal validation of their crushing defeat.

Where is the den of the lions and the feeding place of the young lions, where the lion, lioness and lion's cub prowled, with nothing to disturb *them*? (v. 11).

After Nineveh was plundered, Nahum—in this verse and the next verse—made a mockery or presented a taunt song to the Assyrians. A lion's den is a "feeding" ground for "young lions" and an area where the lion family can roam and eat in an undisturbed manner. The lion imagery is an Assyrian depiction of how they viewed themselves, compared to actual lions. Lions were commonly illustrated in decorations on palace walls throughout the city. The king and queen were portrayed as the "lion" and "lioness," while the "young lions" or young men were depicted as cubs. The Assyrian kings and leaders, who were like lions, prided themselves on the ability to hunt and kill their prey as lions with intrepid fierceness. But an even larger pride of lions had decimated their den and annihilated the entire family.

The lion tore enough for his cubs, killed *enough* for his lionesses, and filled his lairs with prey and his dens with torn flesh (v. 12).

The Ninevites were notorious in the ancient world for their vile, cruel, brutal, and inhumane conquest of other nations and countless enemies. In essence, the Assyrians were lion-like to a degree. A lion, except the hyena, will kill what it wants to eat. The Assyrians not only killed to nourish their own appetite but for the amusement or pleasure of a conquest. While the lion is aggressive, it is not known for enjoyment killing. A lion will kill and not eat a hyena because hyenas are avid killers of lion cubs. Hence, exists their rivalry and hatred for one another. The Assyrians had no provisions—solely a craving for death.

"Behold, I am against you," declares the LORD of hosts. "I will burn up her chariots in smoke, a sword will devour your young lions; I will cut off your prey from the land, and no longer will the voice of your messengers be heard" (v. 13).

It is a dreadful doom when the Lord says, "I am against you" (Jer. 21:13; 50:31; 51:25; Ezek. 5:8; 13:8; 26:3; 28:22; 39:1). The Lord implemented pagan armies as instruments to destroy Nineveh's warfare capabilities; to obliterate the royal family to include the young men ("young lions"); to free the captives from the land—to prohibit the Assyrians from consuming others like a predatory, hungry lion; and to silence the "voice" of their "messengers" forever (2 Kings 18:17-25, 28-35).

Chapter 3

Woe to the bloody city, completely full of lies *and* pillage; *Her* prey never departs (v. 1).

"Woe," which in Hebrew expresses *ah* or *alas*, is an interjection or a lamentation of forthcoming judgment. "Woe" entails grief, misery, sorrow, and other adverse caveats of the Lord's physical reprimand. Nahum declared doom on Nineveh, the city with a warlike nature, which was characterized by bloodshed and enamored with death. Nahum viewed the city as "full of lies" as Rabshakeh, who spoke on behalf of King Sennacherib of Assyria, undermined Hezekiah (2 Kings 18:31-35; 2 Chron. 32:9-15, 17). The power of the Lord prevailed, though, and proved the king of Assyria to be false (2 Kings 19:32-37; 2 Chron. 32:20-21). As stated previously, the Ninevites were pillagers and plunderers (2:9); the city always scavenged for other nations to conquer. Satan—the slanderer—who desires to remove Christians from fellowship and service, "prowls around like a roaring lion, seeking someone to devour" (1 Pet. 5:8). The Ninevites lurked around other populations to dominate and seize them. The contextual difference between this verse and 1 Peter 5:8 is that Nineveh's intention is a total *physical* destruction of its opponents, whereas Satan's objective is to make a *spiritual* ruin of the Christian's relationship with the Lord. However, of course, the devil's goal is literally impossible (Rom 8:1, 31, 37-39).

The noise of the whip, the noise of the rattling of the wheel, galloping horses and bounding chariots! (v. 2).

Nahum describes the sounds and sights of Nineveh's crushing defeat. The whistling slap of the whip; the speedy turning of the chariot wheels; the dashing hoofs of the battle-ready horses; and the leaping chariots in conjunction with a determined calvary of soldiers vividly portray Nineveh's fall. The Lord permitted the prophet to view the slaughter of this city, despite being in the near future.

Horsemen charging, swords flashing, spears gleaming, many slain, a mass of corpses, and countless dead bodies—they stumble over the dead bodies! (v. 3).

The imagery is even more graphic. As horses charged with the resounding thumping as one would hear at the Kentucky Derby in Louisville, Kentucky, or the Pimlico Race Course in Baltimore, Maryland, the battle swords of the horsemen were brightly displayed to slay a myriad of Ninevites while their numerous "corpses" lay in the street. The Ninevite death toll is so massive that the horsemen could not help but "stumble over" them.

***All* because of the many harlotries of the harlot, the charming one, the mistress of sorceries, who sells nations by her harlotries and families by her sorceries (v. 4).**

"All because" signifies the other reason for Nineveh's decimation. Nineveh beheld "harlotries"—leading people into false religion, leading individuals from the truth, and enticing others into sorceries and witchcraft—that contributed to the devastation, as well. The Ninevites practiced sorcery. The Ninevites ensnared other peoples into their wizardries; they betrayed "nations" and "families" and forced them into a lifestyle and culture of occultism, sexual perversion, and human squalor. Additionally, Nineveh lured unsuspecting nations into the act of assisting them with the future intent to harm them. King Ahaz (2 Kings 16:7-18) and King Hezekiah (Isa. 36:16-17) of Judah are prime examples.

"Behold, I am against you," declares the LORD of hosts; "and I will lift up your skirts over your face, and show to the nations your nakedness and to the kingdoms your disgrace (v. 5).

Twice the Lord makes a declaration against Nineveh (2:13), which would experience degradation and shame because of its reprehensible and disgraceful acts. There is a metaphorical contrast of shame as when someone lifted the skirt over a lady's head and covered her face with it (Isa. 47:1-3; Jer. 13:26-27; Ezek. 16:37; Hos. 2:3-5; Rev. 17:15-16). This coarse act exposed a woman's "nakedness" and—in the ancient world—denoted shamefulness. Comparably, the Ninevites, who enslaved other nations with their harlotries (3:4), would have their own "nakedness" unveiled to them.

"I will throw filth on you and make you vile, and set you up as a spectacle (v. 6).

The Lord would cover the Assyrians with detestable abominations (perhaps dung), similar to what they did to other nations, which would identify them as repugnant. He will lift Nineveh up for all to behold its appalling sight.

"And it will come about that all who see you will shrink from you and say, 'Nineveh is devastated! Who will grieve for her?' Where will I seek comforters for you?" (v. 7).

Everyone will withdraw from Nineveh and comment on its "devastated" condition. Nineveh will receive what it surely deserves. People will rejoice, rather than mourn or grieve about its demise. Nineveh will be humiliated before all surrounding nations; and no one will provide it solace.

Are you better than No-amon, which was situated by the waters of the Nile, with water surrounding her, whose rampart *was* the sea, whose wall *consisted* of the sea? (v. 8).

Nineveh was similar to "No-amon," which was the Egyptian capital in Thebes, located in upper southern Egypt. "No-amon" was situated on the Nile River with canals, moats, and tributaries channeling through and surrounding the city, like Nineveh. Such as Nineveh, the city's shoreline provided a water wall for security and fortification. Both cities were capitals of great kingdoms. The staunch defenses of Thebes did not prevail in the end. Likewise, Nineveh's protection would fail.

Ethiopia was *her* might, and Egypt too, without limits. Put and Lubim were among her helpers (v. 9).

"Ethiopia" (or the southern region of contemporary Egypt and northern Sudan, not the present-day Ethiopia), "Put" (in northern Africa, roughly in modern-day Libya), and "Lubim" (in northern Africa, west of Egypt in current Libya) were strong allies of Thebes. Ethiopia, the country over which No-amon ruled, was superior to the other two partners. However, despite all the area coverage that these supporters provided, all three powers combined did not ensure security for Thebes.

Yet she became an exile, she went into captivity; also her small children were dashed to pieces at the head of every street; they cast lots for her honorable men, and all her great men were bound with fetters (v. 10).

Even with these powerful affiliates, Thebes fell to King Ashurbanipal of Assyria in 663 BC, which matched Jeremiah and Ezekiel's predictions (Jer. 46:25; Ezek. 30:14). The Assyrian king "determined on a course of genocide as a way of assuring perpetual submission."[36] The children of Thebes were destroyed, and its "honorable men" experienced the humiliation of being sold into slavery and carted away to Assyria bound in chains.

You too will become drunk, you will be hidden. You too will search for a refuge from the enemy (v. 11).

Literally, extreme inebriation would impair Nineveh's judgment and cause the city to lose its self-governing power; metaphorically, the city would swallow the Lord's cup of wrath that would make it utterly defenseless in battle. Nineveh attempted to hide when it fell, but the Lord had plainly "hidden" the Ninevites from the earth. (See comment on Nahum 1:14.)

> First the ancient capital of Asshur fell in 614 B.C. Then the combined forces of the Medes and the Babylonians assaulted Nineveh in 612 B.C. The city collapsed and was burned after a three-month siege. Retreating toward the west, a remnant of loyal

---

[36] O. Palmer Robertson, *The Books of Nahum, Habakkuk, and Zephaniah: The New International Commentary on the Old Testament Series* (Grand Rapids: Eerdmans Publishing, 1990), 116.

Assyrians established a new king and capital in Harran, approximately 250 miles toward the west. Two years later in 610 B.C., the remaining Assyrian forces were defeated again by Babylon. Although a combined Egyptian and Assyrian force retained some presence in the area for a while, the decisive battle of Carchemish in 605 B.C. eliminated the last vestiges of Assyrian presence in the Fertile Crescent.[37]

All your fortifications are fig trees with ripe fruit—when shaken, they fall into the eater's mouth (v. 12).

Nineveh's "fortifications" (large, imposing walls) are as weak as fig trees laden "with ripe fruit." When "fig trees" are jiggled, the "ripe fruit" falls helplessly into the hungry individual's mouth and is consumed in the stomach. Equally, "when shaken," Ninevites will fall into their attackers' hands, and their invaders, with a sizable appetite, will devour them completely.

Behold, your people are women in your midst! The gates of your land are opened wide to your enemies; fire consumes your gate bars (v. 13).

Regarding the physical weakness of "women," in comparison with the bodily strength of men, the Ninevite soldiers will have exhausted their vigor and prove to be vulnerable and defenseless against their adversaries, contrary to their lionlike image (Isa. 19:16; Jer. 50:37; 51:30). "Although the modern feminist movement may deny it, generally speaking women are weaker physically than men. Particularly when speaking of the hand-to-hand combat of battle, men retain predominance."[38]

---

[37] Ibid., 118-19.

[38] Ibid., 119.

The Ninevites will be unable to prevent the enemy from breaching their gates. The onslaught will be so intense that the soldiers could have left the gates open, as opposed to bolting them shut. Nineveh's foes will not be denied their mission, nor will they be dissuaded from setting the inextinguishable "fire" to the city.

Draw for yourself water for the siege! Strengthen your fortifications! Go into the clay and tread the mortar! Take hold of the brick mold! (v. 14).

This is an alarm call with irony. Despite Sennacherib's aqueduct system, which occupied eighteen canals to stream water into Nineveh, the people would not be able to draw water for themselves. No water supply was in existence for the city. The satirical notion is that Nineveh could utilize bricks to build its walls high and strong enough to withstand the enemies' raid and to employ "mortar" to seal the holes of the attackers' penetrable ramparts.

There fire will consume you, the sword will cut you down; it will consume you as the locust *does*. Multiply yourself like the creeping locust, multiply yourself like the swarming locust (v. 15).

The fire and sword would undoubtedly devastate and destroy the Ninevites. If they somehow were able to fortify their defenses, the "fire"—even if they drew water from some scarce source—would "consume" them. The "sword" would "cut" them "down" as they made a futile effort to reconstruct their battlements.

The destruction to the city would be synonymous with a locust invasion. A mass of military soldiers would invade Nineveh, ravish everything in sight, and leave nothing remaining (Joel 1:2-13). Some scholars suggest that Nahum may refer to the attackers when the command is given to "multiply yourself like the creeping locust…like the swarming locust." If this is true, it convinces the invaders that they will engulf Nineveh and be completely victorious. It seems that this is a continued distress call, though, with an ironical taunt to the city. The words "multiply yourself," which are repeated, are contextually referenced to the Ninevites. They cannot "multiply" their army because of the internal leadership collapse. The "creeping locust" is the caterpillar stage of the Acrididae grasshopper, whereas the "swarming locust" is its flying stage. In any event, whether derisive or not, the conclusion will be the same—Nineveh will be destroyed.

You have increased your traders more than the stars of heaven—the creeping locust strips and flies away (v. 16).

The Assyrian merchants have seemingly multiplied beyond "the stars of heaven," with the city's growing economy, and have immeasurably increased their profits. But when the invaders came, the "traders" took their proceeds, fled, and abandoned Nineveh in vast numbers, compared to "locusts" flying away in a group.

Considered the last great king in Assyria, Ashurbanipal (685-631 BC), for the first time in eight hundred years, dominated western Asia by a sole partisan law: "With the vast territory of the empire under one central government, commerce could flourish throughout this area as never before."[39]

It appears that Nahum's imagery of the wholesalers is quickly transformed from the caterpillar stage of the "creeping locust" to the flying stage of the swarming locust. This depiction could be one of comfortableness to extreme fear during a small window of time.

Your guardsmen are like the swarming locust. Your marshals are like hordes of grasshoppers settling in the stone walls on a cold

---

[39] Walter A. Maier, *The Book of Nahum: A Commentary* (1959; repr., Grand Rapids: Baker Book House, 1980), 348.

day. The sun rises and they flee, and the place where they are is not known (v. 17).

Assyria's "guardsmen" (Hebrew *minzar,* meaning *consecrated ones* or *princes* [though regarding Assyrian culture, the meaning is uncertain]) and "marshals" (city officials)—like the soldiers (3:15) and the traders (3:16)—remind Nahum of locusts, as well. Locusts are known to seek shelter in the crevices and the spots of a wall during the cool of the day but, when the sun rises and beams down on their location, they fly away to a more pleasant environment. Relatedly, these designated men of Assyria will flee from the city to an unknown territory at the opportune time.

Your shepherds are sleeping, O king of Assyria; your nobles are lying down. Your people are scattered on the mountains and there is no one to regather *them* (v. 18).

Nahum specifically addressed King Ashur-uballit, the king of Assyria, who ruled after Nineveh's destruction in 612 BC. Ashur-uballit, who ruled until 609 BC, attempted to maintain the stability of the empire from the city of Haran. The prophet advised the king that his leaders, ironically titled "shepherds" (those who are supposed to teach, care for, and lead the people), and "nobles" (mighty leaders) were in dereliction of their duty by "lying down" on the job and sleeping at the switch. Because the Ninevites were so badly beaten and broken, and the leadership was nonexistent, the common people of the city were "scattered" throughout with "no one to regather them."

There is no relief for your breakdown, your wound is incurable. All who hear about you will clap *their* hands over you, for on whom has not your evil passed continually? (v. 19).

Due to Nineveh's total defeat, the nation of Assyria's "breakdown" would be irreparable. Relief would be to no avail. This would be the Lord's divine, irrevocable judgment. Nineveh's atrocious, evil deeds were manifold, so no one would lift a finger to her aid. Nineveh's prolonged practice of wickedness had affected everyone. The surrounding nations would rejoice in a celebratory fashion over her demise. "Even as the allies hailed the fall of Nazi Germany and the apparent death of Adolf Hitler, so all nations were to greet the news of the demise of Assyria's king."[40]

Like the book of Jonah, Nahum concluded the message of his book with a rhetorical question. Jonah terminates with the remark about the Lord's compassion for the city of Nineveh (Jon. 4:11); Nahum closes with the complete assurance of God's judgment on evil and wicked nations, which viciously and deceitfully subjugate and tyrannize people—especially His people, the Israelites. The Lord's patience had run its course, and Nineveh's judgment of absolute destruction was certain. The sufferers and the oppressed would wait for the Lord's vengeance to occur with the promise of hope, help, and comfort.

---

[40] Robertson, *The Books of Nahum, Habakkuk, and Zephaniah*, 130.

BIBLIOGRAPHY

Alexander, T. D. "Jonah." In *Obadiah, Jonah, and Micah*, 45-131. *The Tyndale Old Testament Commentaries Series*. Downers Grove, IL: InterVarsity Press, 1988.

Allen, Leslie C. *The Books of Joel, Obadiah, Jonah, and Micah: The New International Commentary on the Old Testament Series*. Grand Rapids: Eerdmans Publishing, 1976.

Archer, Gleason L. *A Survey of Old Testament Introduction*. Chicago: Moody Publishers, 2007.

Baker, David W. *Nahum, Habakkuk, and Zephaniah: An Introduction and Commentary*: *The Tyndale Old Testament Commentaries Series*. Downers Grove, IL: InterVarsity Press, 1988.

Baldwin, Joyce. "Jonah." In *The Minor Prophets: An Exegetical and Expositional Commentary*, 2:543-90. 3 vols. Edited by Thomas Edward McComiskey. Grand Rapids: Baker Books, 1998.

Baxter, J. Sidlow. *Explore the Book*. 6 vols. Grand Rapids: Zondervan, 1966.

Chisholm, Robert B., Jr. *Handbook on the Prophets*. Grand Rapids: Baker Book House, 2002.

Feinberg, Charles Lee. *Jonah, Micah, and Nahum. The Major Messages of the Minor Prophets Series*. New York: American Board of Missions to the Jews, 1951.

Fuhr, Al, and Gary Yates. *The Message of the Twelve: Hearing the Voice of the Minor Prophets*. Nashville: B&H Academic, 2016. Kindle.

Gaebelein, Frank E. *Four Minor Prophets: Obadiah, Jonah, Habakkuk, and Haggai*. Chicago: Moody Press, 1970.

Hannah, John D. "Jonah." In *The Bible Knowledge Commentary: Old Testament*, 1461-73. Edited by John F. Walvoord and Roy B. Zuck. Wheaton, IL: Scripture Press Publications, Victor Books, 1985.

Johnson, Elliott E. "Obadiah." In Walvoord and Zuck, 1493–1504.

Kaiser, Walter C., Jr. *Toward an Old Testament Theology*. Grand Rapids: Zondervan Publishing House, 1978.

Longman, Tremper, III. "Nahum." In McComiskey, 2:765–829.

Maier, Walter A. *The Book of Nahum: A Commentary*.1959. Reprint, Grand Rapids: Baker Book House, 1980.

The Merriam-Webster Dictionary: New Edition. Springfield, MA: Merriam-Webster Inc., 2004.

Morgan, G. Campbell. *The Minor Prophets*. Westwood, NJ: Fleming H. Revell, 1960.

The Nelson Study Bible. Edited by Earl Radmacher. Nashville: Thomas Nelson Publishers, 1997.

The New Scofield Reference Bible. Edited by Frank E. Gaebelein, William Culbertson, et al. New York: Oxford University Press, 1967.

Patterson, Richard D. *Nahum, Habakkuk, Zephaniah: Wycliffe Exegetical Commentary Series*. Chicago: Moody Press, 1991.

Robertson, O. Palmer. *The Books of Nahum, Habakkuk, and Zephaniah: The New International Commentary on the Old Testament Series*. Grand Rapids: Eerdmans Publishing, 1990.

Stuart, Douglas. *Hosea-Jonah. Word Biblical Commentary Series*. Waco, TX: Word Books, 1987.

Thrasher, Bill. "Jonah." In *The Moody Bible Commentary*, 1361-68. Edited by Michael Rydelnik and Michael Vanlaningham. Chicago: Moody Publishers, 2014.

Walton, John H. *Zondervan Illustrated Bible Backgrounds Commentary*. 5 vols. Grand Rapids: Zondervan, 2009.

Wiersbe, Warren. *The Bible Exposition Commentary: Isaiah-Malachi*. Colorado Springs: David C. Cook, 2002.

www.ingramcontent.com/pod-product-compliance
Ingram Content Group UK Ltd.
Pitfield, Milton Keynes, MK11 3LW, UK
UKHW040821171224
452492UK00014B/164/J